The Slave-Trader's Children

Also by Gordon Parke:
Coffins for Traitors, Kingfisher Books (1958)
The Early Birds, Kingfisher Books (1963)

THE
SLAVE-TRADER'S
CHILDREN

Gordon Parke

The Book Guild Ltd.
Sussex, England

This book is a work of fiction. The characters and situations in this story are imaginary. No resemblance is intended between these characters and any real persons, either living or dead.

This book is sold subject to the condition that it shall not, by way of trade or otherwise, be lent, re-sold, hired out, photocopied or held in any retrieval system, or otherwise circulated without the publisher's prior consent in any form of binding or cover other than that in which this is published and without a similar condition including this condition being imposed on the subsequent purchaser.

The Book Guild Ltd.
25 High Street,
Lewes, Sussex.

First published 1991
© Gordon Parke 1991
Set in Baskerville
Typesetting by APS,
Salisbury, Wiltshire.
Printed in Great Britain by
Antony Rowe Ltd.,
Chippenham, Wiltshire.
British Library Cataloguing in Publication Data
Parke, Gordon
The slave-trader's children
I. Title
823.914 [J]

ISBN 0 86332 587 4

1

This is the story of Richard and Selina, children of a slave-trading family.

Their mother was one of the three Crossman girls, Katharine who was born in 1711, Peggy born in 1713 and Sarah after another two years.

They were born into a rich, respectable slave-trading family and lived in a fine solid, square house in Whitechapel in the suburbs of London.

Katharine was the tallest and most handsome, Peggy was beautiful and serious and Sarah was pretty with a smiling face. If the truth were told Mr Crossman had always wanted a son to carry on the business. Nevertheless he loved his daughters and his business was going to have a great effect on all three girls.

Katharine married Sir Adam Kilmore who was himself the heir to a slave-trading company. Mr Crossman gladly paid a dowry and gave a share of his business to Sir Adam. For whereas Mr Crossman had had to work to keep his business going, Sir Adam was a gentleman and did not work. Katharine went to live in Kilmore House in Sussex, and in 1735 a son, George, was born to them.

Peggy loved work and travelled to Liverpool and Bristol to choose sea captains to run their ships and slave traders to work in Africa. To her father's disappointment she chose to marry one of these slave-traders, Henry Calvert. He was no gentleman and before applying for the job had been working with cattle on the farm. With Peggy's help he established a slave-trading post at the mouth of the Camaranca river in Sierra Leone. They had two children, Richard, born in the same year as his cousin George, and Selina who was born in 1737.

Sarah had many admirers, but also an independence of spirit. Perhaps it was this that stopped her marrying or perhaps she felt it right to stay in Whitechapel to look after her mother and father till their deaths in 1740 and 1742. She was a good daughter, a good sister and, more important in our story, a good aunt.

She often went to Kilmore House to see George, and though she had never seen Richard and Selina, she wrote to them and received letters in return. She still lived in Whitechapel, and received her income from the slave-trading company though she did not work for it as Peggy did.

An earnest, young man who had once wooed her asked whether it was right to take away the liberty from men, women and children and to make them slaves. There had been a hush round the shocked Crossman family as they sat eating heartily. Then Sarah had replied that by purchasing or rather, ransoming the negroes from the national chiefs or kings and by transplanting them to a civilized country with the kindly influences of the law and the gospel, these negroes were granted a much greater degree of happiness, though admittedly not to absolute liberty.

After the meal the suitor was ushered out. Never had the seventeen year old Sarah been so popular.

Unfortunately this popularity was not to last.

2

Peggy was never happy if she was not working, and any success Henry Calvert had had was largely due to her. She had an ability to concentrate on what was important and to remember everything she had learned. She taught her children 'Duty first, duty second; then it's time for pleasure.' In some ways it never was time for pleasure with her children, but they were not unhappy.

Every morning Richard and Selina were given their duties to do. These would include school work, but also many duties about their log built house on the coast of Sierra Leone.

When Sarah read to Katharine an uncomplaining letter she had received from Richard, the mistress of Kilmore House said, 'I can't understand it. Peggy has plenty of slaves. Why should Richard and Selina do the cleaning?'

Sarah laughed.

'You're forgetting what Peggy was like. We had plenty of servants, but Peggy's room was always beautiful because she made it so.'

'I still wish she had not married Henry Calvert. He is no gentleman.'

'Perhaps it is better to be married to Henry rather than to be married to no-on at all.'

'Well, Sarah,' said the helpful Katharine. 'I can find plenty of gentlemen who will be interested in you with your income.'

Sarah laughed again.

3

Peggy and Henry had found the ideal place for their African slave factory. It was at the mouth of the Camaranca which provided easy access to the jungle villages. There was a flat grassy plain between the trees and the river, and slave ships could anchor a quarter of a mile off shore. Their home built by slaves was sturdy. The walls were of coconut tree logs and the roof was thatched with banana leaves which provided good protection from the sweltering sun and the pelting rain. The central hut was where they lived and ate. There were smaller huts for sleeping, cooking and for goods they would use for bartering with village chiefs for slaves.

Henry was often away from home in his shallop a shallow-draughted boat. He sailed up the coast and up the Camaranca. Peggy made the plans. She had trained some of her house slaves to provide the best postal service the white traders knew. The African chiefs had their own methods of communication which were just as effective.

Neither Richard nor Selina knew their father well. Richard respected him, but he was old enough to realize they both found it difficult to talk to one another. Henry spent his time with his guns. He loved and tended these; he never did the same to his children.

If Richard and Selina went to him, he would reply, 'Ask your mother,' or 'Do as your mother says.'

Richard couldn't remember his father or mother ever doing anything together. Selina had once told him that mother had said, 'The trouble is your father's not a gentleman.'

They pondered what this meant and at the time they felt it suggested their father was rough. He had never seemed rough to them. If anything mother was rougher.

One day some excitement broke their normal routine. Sam, their chief and trusted house slave had learnt there was much honey not far upstream. Honey was a luxury. Peggy quickly organized a party headed by Sam to collect some. Their ass had three containers roped on either side of him.

Then Peggy saw her children waiting for lessons. Peggy had a headache and had not been well.

'It is time you were useful,' she said. 'Go with Sam and learn how to find and collect honey.'

While Sam and the two other slaves were with difficulty coaxing the ass on to the large flat rowing boat, Peggy came out and said to Richard, 'Watch the slaves. I do not want any escaping.'

Richard was pleased and took the warning seriously. Now that he was ten he must look after the family property.

The slaves paddled slowly upstream with the jungle seeming to try to trample them under with its mangrove feet. Selina going on the river for the first time found the darkness and the overhanging trees frightening. After two miles Sam beached the boat at a small clearing. They pushed the ass, who was now showing no enthusiasm for leaving the boat, ashore. The slaves grabbed their containers and led by Sam they crossed the clearing and entered a narrow overhung path. They could hear a buzz. Richard and Selina followed holding hands.

The buzz grew louder. Their path widened to a larger clearing. Sam stood still. Then he turned and told the slaves to go back. At the same moment a swarm of bees half filled the clearing, shutting out the sun. The fierce native bees zoomed like small bullets towards them. Richard felt the roar of the wings of a thousand bees as the slaves in front turned and fled past them. Richard pulling Selina ran back through the pathway.

There were bees all over them. Crying and panting they reached the boat. The two slaves were there beating off the bees, but all were stung with jabs of pain on all their bare flesh. Sam appeared, but there was no ass.

The children crawled on to the boat crying, and the slaves managed painfully to row them home.

There was no sympathy from their mother. She beat them both in spite of their stings and sent them to bed. She had Sam and the two slaves fasted by chains to their ankles to large posts outside. They were given no food or water for the rest of the day.

Richard and Selina were not sorry for Sam and the slaves. They weren't even particularly sorry for themselves. This was life for them at Camaranca.

4

Sir Adam Kilmore looked from his fine house with some satisfaction. It was a house of splendour and success as it stood proudly over the fields of Barcombe. He felt that his house had the character of a gentleman.

He looked at the garden, where four gardeners, perhaps conscious of his figure at the window, were labouring. Even Sir Charles Marsh, the magistrate at nearby Newick could not better that, he considered. He smoothed the waistcoat over his middle, which was increasing as years went by. Yet he was only forty-four, respected by all who mattered, and with many prosperous years of life stretching before him.

Life, however was not perfect.

The lesser of his worries had been the news of a battle which had reached him in which Bonnie Prince Charlie had been defeated in Scotland. Sir Adam was a Tory and a Jacobite at heart. The Stuarts across the water knew this and his reward would be deservedly great when they came into their own again.

However he was careful to keep his beliefs to himself except after a few brandys with friends of similar views. Then he would rail against 'the Hanover pig, who can't control his wife and can't speak English.' Sir Adam enjoyed the thought of standing up to persecution, though, if the truth be told, he had not had to suffer much yet.

His greater worry was money, or rather the lack of it. When he had married Katharine, two noble slave-trading companies had been linked together and prosperity should have been assured, had not the Kilmore Company had the most appalling bad luck with incompetent captains, who allowed too many slaves to die on the passage to the West Indies.

His wife entered the room. She clutched a letter. Sir Adam's spirits rose again. His wife was still beautiful, was wonderful at running a house and he did not forget past favours; her dowry had meant he could keep the family house in the proper style.

'Sir Adam,' she called, always using his title, 'I've received a letter and money from Peggy. All goes well at the factory, and she wants to buy a new slave ship. Shall you ask Captain Manesty to order one at Rhode Island again?'

Sir Adam's views were not in fact needed, but his wife loyally asked him.

'They are colonials, but they are also cheap; much cheaper than Liverpool. Did your sister send all the money for it?'

'Yes, and more than that, she's sent enough for a year's school fees for Richard and Selina.'

'We must proceed with caution, Lady Katharine. Parson Chipperfield is fine at teaching George. He could manage two more without any extra pay I would wager.'

'But, Sir Adam, if I said we would send them to school . . . .'

'I think Lady Katharine, you can leave that to me. Beggars cannot be choosers.'

He stopped. He saw the magistrate from Newick come trotting in through the gates.

'Sir Charles is coming. I shall go to meet him.'

As he walked through his front door he was conscious that in this meeting lay a greater worry than the defeat of the Jacobites or the arrival of his nephew and niece.

5

Captain Sebastian Clow was the nearest slave-trading neighbour to the Calverts. His claim to be a captain was generally doubted; certainly he spoke with considerable dislike about the army. However, he had now become a rich man after arriving penniless from England. He owned a share in a slave ship and hoped to build another slave factory near the Calverts at Camaranca. His log-cabin home in the plantains was impressively large and built on a sandy island just off shore ten miles south of the Calverts. His huts were bigger than the Calverts' and his special pride was his long barn with its rows of upright posts and chains and padlocks. This was the final resting place in Africa for the sad lines of slaves who had trekked for many miles and had been brought in by Clow's fleet of canoes.

But recently Clow had had too many empty posts. He could not find enough slaves. He made two moves to remedy this. He signed on an English assistant, who had been anxious to leave his slave ship. Previously he had served in the navy. Clow gathered from the slave's ship's captain that he had won no glory in either. Clow did not care. It gave him the opportunity to offer much lower pay than usual.

'There was little in his favour except that he was white.' Clow explained to Henry Calvert. 'He's a fighter, but a fighter may be valuable. And he can handle ships. I shall give him a trial as I go North.'

Then came Clow's second move.

'I am going to marry a princess,' he added as casually as he could.

Henry knew this. Gossip travelled as fast in Sierra Leone as in Sussex. She was a black princess; she came from the tribe who had first sold Clow slaves.

Peggy Calvert said to Henry, 'Sebastian Clow will be finished. He can never be a gentleman now; not even when he returns home. The respect due to his profession will be lost if he marries a jungle-bred black.'

'I shall see her tomorrow,' said Henry. 'I am rowing to the Plantains to see Sebastian before he goes north again. He told me he might have found a new village with many slaves.'

'I expect the news was part of the dowry,' said Peggy uncharitably. 'Take the children with you. Mrs Clow might like them.'

Henry was surprised. Every day Peggy taught the children to read, write and count. This was an unchanging rule. He looked at his wife closely. She was not well.

'Are you well?' he asked.

'Of course I am well. The children must learn the trade. They will go with you.'

The children were excited and surprised. Rarely had they missed lessons before, and never had they seen any other slave factories.

'It will be the first morning ever that we have not had lessons,' shouted Richard not altogether accurately.

'I think mother is tired,' replied Selina more accurately.

The journey to the Plantains was not easy. With four house slaves rowing their large boat took well over two hours, but for Richard and Selina it was bliss. They were soon lightly tossing on the boat as they crossed the estuary. They slapped their hands in the water. They splashed one another and the slaves. They peered in the water at the river mouth and saw fishes they had never seen before. They pushed one another and argued. Their father sat silently at the prow of the boat. He didn't interfere.

They discussed Mr Clow and his princess wife. They could not imagine a white man with a black wife.

'Would she be wearing any clothes?' Selina wondered. 'The black slaves didn't.'

'She'll be the first princess I've ever seen,' said Richard still caught up with the magic of the word.

'But she's black,' objected Selina.

Their father didn't speak. He wanted to talk with Sebastian about his next trip inland and to swap information on new slave-hunting grounds. He was interested in seeing his new white assistant. He had no desire to meet his new wife.

The boat bumped gently against the short wooded jetty that

stretched into the river. Richard and Selina jumped nimbly on to the jetty while their father clambered up beside them.

Sebastian usually came to meet him, but the dry mud track up to the house was empty. Then Henry noticed that the Clow's shallop, which was used for trading, was not moored at its usual berth. Sebastian must have left earlier. It had been a wasted trip. Then Henry reflected that perhaps he should meet this princess wife; Peggy would certainly be curious.

He stepped towards the house to pay his respects. The hard, bare feet of the children scampered over the mud and reached the hut.

6

Lady Katharine Kilmore was examining the accounts. Publicly, all financial affairs were left to the husband, but Sir Adam never having been short of money found it hard to bother with them all.

She was puzzled. There seemed to be no money coming from the Kilmore Trading Company. The Crossmans' money was keeping Kilmore House going. Peggy in particular was contributing. Although it was sad that she had not married a gentleman, she clearly had the Crossmans' money-making abilities. Since the reign of Charles II both families had been members of the Royal African Company which held the monopoly for slave-trading, but whereas the Crossmans thrived, the Kilmores seemed to be failing.

She had passed on her worries to Sir Adam, but he merely blamed her for fussing and said the money would come. Then that morning he had handed her one hundred pounds in notes. It had not come from the Kilmore Trading Company. It was possible it had been won on bets, but if that were so, why had Sir Adam handed it over with no boasting about his prowess at cards or horses? He usually did.

Her mind them moved on to Sarah. She had always in the past been a great enthusiast for the family company and like Peggy had often travelled to Bristol and Liverpool. Now she had changed.

'The devil's got her with religion,' said Sir Adam, and it says a lot for Katharine as a wife that she still believed nearly all her husband said.

Katharine decided to talk to Sarah when she next came. Some of her money was needed in Kilmore House.

She heard the voices of Sir Adam and his magistrate neighbour from Newick, Sir Charles Marsh. Katharine had wondered whether this meeting was concerned with money,

16

and whether Sir Charles had been lending money. Certainly she had noticed that Sir Adam had been strangely uneasy before the visit.

Sir Charles was a confident man. He had had a successful career in the army and was a friend of the Duke of Newcastle another Sussex neighbour, the most powerful man in Walpole's government.

'We shall need your help again, Adam,' he said. 'There is a new riding officer. He came to me as the local Justice of the Peace and said that information had been received about smuggled goods at the Sloop Inn. I gave him permission to take his dragoons which were stationed at Cuckfield to inspect them. Needless to say when he arrived they found nothing. Jebb gave the officer and his men a drink, and they left happy. As the officer rode with me back to Newick he said that he felt it would be worth watching the Sloop closely. It seems this captain is not a fool.'

'Jebb could deal with him,' said Adam, who foresaw how the conversation was going.

'Yes, but remember there are dragoons as well; there is also possibly an informer that we have to root out. Now I think this captain will turn out to be a man we can buy, but it is sense to leave the Sloop empty and to plant our seed elsewhere for a short season. I have one thousand pounds of tea arriving this week. I have indeed already sold it to the London traders. It must stay at Kilmore House until my carriers come.'

Fear and greed fought in Adam's mind. Sir Charles sensed his hesitation.

'If the free traders have used your splendid house once, as indeed they have, it is no more dangerous and much more profitable if they come again.'

Sir Charles departed. Adam envied his assurance. He called for Jacob, his head gardener, to give instructions.

7

The princess watched the Calverts arrive. She knew who they were. They were the main rivals to the Clows. They too wanted the best slaves. The princess had learnt early in life that there was no place for rivals. She was the most intelligent, and the most courageous of the chief's children. She understood most of all what it meant to be chief. She worked with her father. Her brothers appreciated that she was a rival even though she was a girl. They persuaded her father she must be married to the son of the richest member of the tribe, and must in no way be a rival to the sons' hope for power.

The princess, aged fifteen, was one of the few girls of eighteenth century Africa who succeeded in defying her father's proposal. As the chief enjoyed her company, and profited greatly from her success in supplying slaves to traders he showed unusual patience and for four years she succeeded in putting off the marriage. The chief was undisturbed. He was becoming richer through her efforts, and he knew he would have his will in the end.

But he was wrong. One day the princess departed with the white slave-trader, Sebastian Clow.

The princess realized where the power lay. She took with her her beauty, her ruthlessness, her knowledge of the slave trade, her own slaves, her money and still, strangely enough the love of her father.

She had not much time for Sebastian, though she recognized that, as he was a white slave-trader, through him she could build up an empire that would outshine her father's or rather her brothers'.

Her new home, though no worse than her tribal home, would in time become a palace such as she had seen the Portuguese slave-traders build.

Her own slaves smartly replaced Sebastian's, who were

shipped on the next slaver across the Atlantic. She was still treated as a princess. No-one had ever dared to call her Mrs Clow, and with good reason.

Sebastian's success had been due to his work up the coast, much helped by the princess and her local knowledge. She knew that this source was diminishing. All the criminals, the opponents, the poor farmers and their families and the conquered had already disappeared in long coffles to Sebastian's factories. Further riches lay in the tribes inland and it was here that Henry Calvert worked. He was an unwanted rival.

The Calverts found the door closed. Henry was puzzled. It had never been closed before. He strode up and banged on the door. There was a pause of some fifteen seconds before the door opened and a bald slave bowed before Henry, and stood back for him to enter followed by the two children. They were led into what had been Sebastian's dining room. In it had been a makeshift wooden table and four wooden chairs; that was all. Henry stopped in the doorway by the slave. He looked in amazed. The walls were all draped in brightly coloured cloths, the floor was covered by a fine carpet (the first that Richard and Selina had ever seen), the table with six carved legs shone in black and at the far end there was a dais three feet high with steps in front.

On the dais was a throne in the same black wood inset with ivory. On the throne sat the princess with a beauty and an authority shining from her more brightly than the ivory gleaming on the throne.

She wore, Selina remembered later, a white African dress, with red bracelets and earrings, and three ringed multi-coloured necklaces.

The bald slave put out his hand and stopped Henry before entering.

'Stop before the steps. Bow down to the Princess.' He took back his hand. 'Do not say a word.'

Henry's mind was awhirl. The transformed room and the princess made him gasp. Then to be stopped by a slave; to be told what to do by a slave; to be told to bow to a negro and to be told to be silent. Nothing in his life had prepared him for this. Yet he stepped forward and stopped before the steps. He could not bow, but then the power and beauty before him overcame him and he got as far towards a bow as he could –

slow nod of the head. The princess's face seemed to harden, but Selina and Richard on either side of their father realized that they too must show their respects.

Richard gave a splendid bow he had been taught ready for his life in England, and Selina curtseyed with grace.

The princess's expression relaxed.

'Rise,' she said.

When Richard thought back about this he had to add one more accomplishment to the princess. She must have been able to read. This was what an English princess would say, even though it was not very applicable at that time.

The princess's mind was working fast. How could she best rid Africa of the Calverts. Two ideas came into her mind. She rose.

'Welcome,' she said. 'Captain Clow is away, but I can talk about the trade in a way that will be profitable for you.' She motioned to Henry to sit down by the table.

'I will return soon,' she said to him. 'Come with me, children.' She led them outside. She had planned this to be an important day in her life.

8

An important day in Sarah Crossman's life had taken place some three years earlier in 1742.

Her father had died that summer. In the last week of his life he had told Sarah that now it was time for her to marry a gentleman. Up till that moment he had been very against any such thing, and indeed Sarah herself had considered it her duty to look after the ageing old man.

She had plenty of money, some devoted servants, and a fine house built by her father that led onto the Great Garden at Whitechapel. She discovered the joys of London life, the theatre, the circuses, and the balls, and she usually attended church on Sunday, as all respectable ladies did.

She loved reading. When she wandered into a bookshop in the High Street she found a copy of one of William Hogarth's pictures called, 'The Sleeping Congregation.' She clapped her hands in delight. 'It's just like our church,' she said and bought it for a shilling. She took it home and showed it to her housekeeper and dearest friend, Mrs Collington.

As her housekeeper looked at the congregation all asleep in the picture and the vicar droning on through page after page of his papers with the help of a magnifying glass, she wasn't sure how to please her mistress. Should she be shocked, or should she laugh as she wanted to?

Luckily Sarah laughed first, and so did Mrs Collington.

Next day was Sunday and Sarah overslept.

'I've had enough sleeping now,' she said merrily to her maid, Sophia, who was attending to her hair. Sarah thought how glorious it was not to be responsible to anyone.

'I don't need any sleeping in church today!'

After Sarah had eaten she looked across the Great Gardens, and saw it was filling not with the ladies and gentlemen of fashion, and the respectable tradesmen who hoped to be the

21

ladies and gentlemen of fashion enjoying a Sunday stroll, but with a great rabble of women and men who clearly were neither ladies nor gentlemen.

'Who are these?' she inquired holding up a beautifully powdered hand at the window.

'John Wesley, the preacher comes to speak in the Great Gardens this afternoon, ma'am,' replied Mrs Collington.

'I have heard that Mr Wesley makes a great noise in the country,' said Sarah. 'The Rector of Barcombe speaks against him.'

'I heard them sing a song in the tavern:
"John Wesley is come to town,
To try to pull the churches down",' interrupted Sophia.

'Be quiet, Sophia,' said Mrs Collington sharply. 'My brother heard Mr Wesley speak at Moorfields and said he spoke like an angel.'

'The Vicar said he was an enthusiast, and that he would not allow an enthusiast to speak in the church,' said Sarah.

Sarah's smile stopped Mrs Collington's reproach.

'We shall go to hear Mr Wesley,' announced Sarah. 'Fetch my coat and hat, Sophia.'

9

The princess led the children outside down towards the jetty.
'You like to play in the sea?' she asked.

They nodded.

'Play here by the jetty.'

'We are not allowed to,' said Richard. 'Crocodiles.'

'It is safe,' she said, 'crocodiles do not like the sea. You will like it.'

Richard thought it looked like a river, but he saw that round the other sides from the jetty were fixed large trunks making an inner pool. His desire to jump in linked with his desire to obey the princess.

'I will come back when I have talked with your father.' She turned and moved gracefully indoors.

Richard and Selina looked at one another. Then they laughed, stripped off their clothes, and fell happily into the water. It was warm and refreshing. Bliss slid over the children as the water did. They could not swim but the water was not deep. As Richard strode out it only reached his chest as he came to the barricade.

He went back to splash Selina who was tumbling happily near the edge. Selina chased Richard back into the stream.

'Let's try to swim,' said Richard.

They tried without much success. They roared with laughter.

Selina rubbing her eyes looked back towards the house.

'I think the princess is looking at us,' she spluttered.

'I can't see her,' said Richard.

'No, she has gone now.'

Richard ducked under the water and came up looking the other way. He saw the wooden barricade with a large log on top. He rubbed the muddy water from his face. The big log had eyes.

'Selina,' he screamed, grabbing her. 'Out, come out. There's a crocodile.'

Hand in hand they scrambled to the bank and they heard the splash behind them.

They ran up the bank and flopped by their clothes. Richard dared to look round. There in the middle of the low enclosure was a scaly crocodile, its eyes just above the waterline watching them.

The crocodile winked. The children stared. Then Richard winked and laughed. Selina laughed.

'Let's get dressed,' said Richard.

'She's watching again,' said Selina, and she was not talking about the crocodile.

10

Never before had the Great Gardens of Whitechapel been so full as on the afternoon of 12th September 1742. Cock-fighting was popular and attracted a hundred or two. It was home territory for Whitechapel Warlord who many times, blood-splattered but triumphant, had raised cheers from his supporters who laid their money on his steel-spurred legs.

The Gentlemen of Kent had played one of the newer manly pastimes of cricket against Lord Montford's team. Sarah had been taken by his Lordship's son, and had watched with surprise gentlemen playing with blacksmiths, and the great Lord Montford seriously defending two sticks with a curved bat. The spectators including Sarah's companion were busy betting. After the game which the Gentlemen of Kent won, Sarah was about to ask a disgruntled Lord Montford about this puzzling game of cricket when he pronounced, 'Cricket is a game foreigners can never understand.'

Sarah didn't ask her questions.

As Sarah, Mrs Collington and Sophia walked from the road across the grass, they found themselves in a pushing crowd making towards the centre of the Gardens.

'Shall we turn back?' asked Mrs Collington, suddenly realizing she had caused Sarah to come. 'There are more unwashed villains here than you'll find in Bedlam.'

Sarah had never been in a crowd like this. Ladies did not mingle in common crowds. She remembered the cricket match. There must have been two hundred people there and ten times that here.

'We shall go on,' she said firmly. 'If this Mr Wesley can draw so many more than the Great Lord Montford, then he must be worth hearing, though I cannot say that I'm impressed with his supporters.'

'I don't think they are all his supporters ma'am,' said the

excited Sophia who was loving it. 'They haven't got prayer books in their hands; they've got stones.'

'The girl could be right,' muttered Mrs Collington, for she sensed her mistress's intentions and walked in front shouting. 'clear the way for my lady.' The people did.

They walked across the grass to an uneven platform of logs laid on stumps, some three feet high. No-one was on it. Sarah was standing nearly in the front row protected by her servants.

The noise grew louder as three black coated men mounted the platform.

'He looks like a gentleman,' said Sarah.

Wesley wore no wig, but his dark hair stretched down to his shoulders. Only the white preaching tabs under his chin relieved his black gown.

'Hold steady with the stones,' grunted a harsh voice behind them. 'Do not throw till I give the word. If you hit the blaspheming wretch your shillings will double. And if this wailing Wesley never visits Whitechapel again the Parson promises more to come, and so does Farmer Walter.'

Sarah looked round in horror. A coarse, dirty and powerful group of men were gazing at the group on the platform with murmuring rage. In their hands were stones.

John Wesley began to speak.

11

The Ouse meandered across ill-kept Sussex meadows from Ashdown Forest through the Downs at Lewes and then by even rougher fields to Newhaven and the sea. Kent and Sussex have a coastline of more than two hundred miles, and in 1745 this brought more joy to smugglers than to holiday makers.

Walpole and his parliament had hoped that customs duties would be gold eggs from a goose, that would raise little protest from the rich or poor. After all, the Whigs argued, it was luxuries they were taxing, and no-one would starve without them. Thus immediate and easy returns would come from their duties on tea, coffee, rum, brandy, tobacco and fine fabrics. Year by year the government attempted to reduce the national debt by increasing customs duties. Thus tea when bought in London would incur duty of seventy-five percent. The higher the customs duties went, the more smuggling was encouraged. The harsher the punishments inflicted for stealing, the more ruthless were the tactics of smugglers.

Few in Kent or Sussex would have thought of giving evidence against a smuggler, and the magistrates and gentlemen themselves were often more than mere spectators.

The easy earning of £200 had brought Sir Adam into the smuggling fraternity, and once in, the only way out was death.

Behind Kilmore House there was a terrace from which steps led down to a field. A hundred yards from the hall lay the Garden House proudly erected by Sir Adam, and ten yards beyond that the River Ouse.

☆   ☆   ☆

Henry had had the most difficult half an hour of his life. Even an angry wife was nothing like so frightening as this black princess. And this had happened when he came on a friendly visit to see Sebastian and as he secretly thought to have a laugh with Sebastian over his marrying an African. Henry had put the marriage down purely to financial and business advantages.

The princess could speak broken English. She made it clear what part of the territory she regarded as providing slaves for the Clows. She asked about Henry's intentions.

Henry was doubtful as to how much information he should give. He was disconcerted by her aggression, her walking round as she talked, her gazing out of the window, and then the sudden return to her throne.

She then mentioned King Ambo. She knew that this king had an abundant supply of slaves from his raids on neighbouring tribes and from his criminals. It required a journey twenty miles upstream in his shallop. The princess turned round from the window. She strode back to the throne. She faced Henry, her face shining with interest.

'I know much about King Ambo,' she said. 'Many slaves and good ivory. But you must heed well what I say. If you do not heed my words there will be much trouble. You understand?'

'I shall hear your words,' said Henry.

'You will heed me. You will heed me,' her voice rose.

'Yes,' said Henry uncomfortable and alarmed.

'Do not sell King Ambo guns. You understand? No guns. Take cloth, take knives, take drinks, but no guns. Danger to you if he has guns. Great danger to you. You understand? No guns to King Ambo.'

'He will want guns,' said Henry, but seeing an anger rise in the princess he added, 'but I will remember. Perhaps he will like the rum.'

'No guns, no guns,' she repeated.

Henry wanted to change the subject.

'Has your assistant gone in the shallop with your husband?'

The princess was silent for a time. She gave no sign of having heard the question.

'You take my words. I will help you. You will get many slaves from King Ambo, but give him no guns. Come with me.'

12

'Our Lord said to us, "Repent and believe the Gospel",' said John Wesley.

Sarah looked and listened. 'He is a gentleman,' she remarked to Mrs Collington. 'He speaks as a gentleman.'

At first the crowd were quiet, but soon murmurs and then shouts made it more difficult to hear his words. John Wesley's voice still rang out ignoring the insults.

Sarah was enjoying it all. It was not so much Wesley's words for by now she was only half listening. It was the excitement of the atmosphere. The dark-gowned gentleman spoke with authority and yet all around him were many who wished him ill. Sarah loved to be thrilled. She had often wished she had gone to Sierra Leone with Peggy, or married a fine gentleman and had run a great house like Katharine, but at this moment she would have been nowhere but in the Great Gardens of Whitechapel. Here indeed was drama, far more exciting than the amusements of Congreve in the theatre. Then she saw a movement of the crowd on the other side of the stage. A pathway was opening. Through it a herd of cows was being driven toward Wesley's platform. Farm hands were shouting behind them and driving them on with whips. The cattle lurched forward mooing.

'Let's move, Miss Crossman,' screamed Sophia. 'The bulls will be on us.'

Sarah did not move, but for the first time the shouts of the crowd and the lowing of the herd stopped Mr Wesley's voice.

13

Richard and Selina trotted back to the house. They both sensed that it would be wise if their short swim remained a secret. Their father might not be angry, but their mother certainly would.

They reached the front door. A slave was standing there and stepped in front.

'No,' he said. 'Do not go in.'

Richard looked at him in surprise.

'Why not?' he asked. 'We are going to see our father.'

'No,' he said firmly. 'The princess say for you not to go in. You wait.'

Richard like his father did not enjoy being told what to do by slaves. Yet the house and all that had happened made him feel uneasy. The influence of the princess in particular was powerful and threatening.

'Come on,' interrupted Selina. 'Let's be explorers.'

☆   ☆   ☆

The cattle were within ten yards of the platform. John Wesley's two companions stood beside him and seemed to be urging him to retreat.

'Dissenting pig, dissenting pig!' shouted a rough voice just behind Sarah.

'Chase him, chase him,' shouted another voice, though it was not clear whether he was addressing the cows or the congregation.

The people near the cattle were drawing away in alarm, when the leading cows lurched to a stop and then charged round and started going back. The other cows mooed loudly and stopped and turned too. The farm hands stopped too in amazement and then rushed sideways into the crowd as the

herd thundered back towards them.

'They are going,' gasped trembling Sophia.

'It is a miracle,' announced Mrs Collington firmly.

'The religion of Christ is infinitely higher and deeper than the most excellent church ceremonies,' said Mr Wesley to his moving congregation.

'Away with him,' shouted Curate Kitson who loved church ceremonies above all else. 'Do not hear the scoundrel who wants to destroy the church.'

'You may have great knowledge,' called out Mr Wesley, 'and still be a stranger to the religion of the heart.'

'Mr Wesley hardly stops talking whatever happens,' remarked Sarah to Mrs Collington.

'But I do believe he means what he says.' Sarah was interested.

The crowd was quieter now except for the group in front of Sarah who were being passed further ammunition in small sacks. The voice of Wesley was still ringing out with the background of lowing from the retreating cattle.

Sarah began to listen more. She enjoyed the touches of humour and the logic of his arguments. The crowd was again a congregation and congregations listen when they sense authority whether the authority is good or bad.

'Spread round behind him. Take this sack of stones,' said the rough voice that had been silent for a while. Then the voice grew louder.

'Down with Methodisty dogs, down with Methodisty dogs.'

The cry was taken up.

The leader threw a stone.

'Out of the way, lass,' said another pushing Sophia to one side. Another large stone whistled through the air straight at Mr Wesley.

14

The exploration of Richard and Selina was disappointing. Their first call was to the kitchen. They had always found house-slaves kind to them. They knew a kitchen was a good place in which to find kindness.

But this time when they arrived there was no kindness – just scowls. Perhaps they were frightened scowls, but the message was clear.

'Don't come in. Go away. Go away.'

So Richard and Selina began to investigate the other huts. They were locked, but the children peering between the logs could see barrels of rum, knives, rolls of cloth and guns. They knew what these were for. They had huts like this in their Camaranca home. They were to be used for trading with the African chiefs. In return would come slaves.

Then they came to some large shelters thinly walled on three sides with banana leaves interlapping one another as a roof. There were posts with chains and padlocks on in rows.

'They have no slaves,' said Selina.

'Perhaps that is why the princess is in such a bad temper,' replied Richard. 'Mr Clow must be up river collecting more.'

They wandered on reaching at last a more dilapidated shelter, with a sagging roof. It was near the river.

'Here are the slaves,' remarked Selina. 'I can hear chains. Listen.'

They walked round the side wall and looked cautiously in.

It was dark after the sunlight and all the children could see were the jagged patches where the sun pierced the withering roof.

'No, it's empty,' said Richard looking at some of the slave posts dappled in the sun. And then they heard a clink of a chain again. They looked into a far dark corner.

'There is a slave over there. He's not chained to a post. Look,

he is lying on that box.' Selina pointed, and Richard could see something move.

'Careful,' he said. 'He might be a dangerous slave if he's all on his own.' They crept forward with their eyes growing accustomed to the dim light.

They saw a man lying on a mat which covered a seaman's chest. His head lay on a palm log. He wore a torn white cotton shirt and trousers which were ripped off just below the knees. His ankles were attached by a link chain two feet long which rattled as the man tossed and turned.

Selina and Richard looked at one another in amazement, as they stood by the log.

'He's white,' they both gasped together.

As they spoke the man heaved and turned over towards them. The children stepped back. The man opened his eyes and stared blankly at them. He raised his hand and brushed it over his eyes. He looked at the two small figures in white.

'You are real then. Real white children,' he muttered. 'I thought that damned she-devil was casting her spells over me.'

Selina did not like the look of him. Richard was thinking hard. Hadn't he heard his father say that Mr Clow was getting a new white assistant. But no white assistant would be treated like this. And yet he couldn't have a white slave.

'Come over here, girl. Let me touch you.'

'No,' said Richard. 'Don't go.'

Selina had had no intention of going and clasped her brother's hand.

The man tossed and turned and grasped his forehead with his two hands.

'Water,' he croaked. 'Water, bring me water.'

The children turned and went out of the hut. The sunshine warmed and cheered them.

'He's white,' said Richard. 'What is he doing in there?'

'He's ill,' replied Selina sitting down by a palm tree and watching the river. 'Perhaps that's where they look after ill people.'

'They are not looking after him. I think he's dying,' said Richard. 'He's dying from the river fever,' he added remembering words of his mother.

'He doesn't like the princess,' said Selina.

'Nor do I,' said Richard and added boldly, 'I'm going to get him some water. There was a bowl lying by his bed. I'll get some water from the river in that. You remain here, Selina.'

Richard walked back into the hut.

36

15

The first stone struck the back of John Wesley's coat a glancing blow, bounced on the platform and then onto the grass of the Great Gardens in front of those who had regained their places when the cattle had retreated. More stones flew from other parts of the crowd, but the greatest and closest battery came from the gang who were milling just by Sarah.

She turned angrily on them. Her dress and her appearance gave her a brief authority which held them back. Then the greatest shouter seized Sophia and threw her aside. The rest followed him. They were now in the front row. Sarah was helping Sophia up. Mrs Collington was hitting their backs with her fists.

John Wesley's companions raised their arms to protect their heads, but they stood firm by John, who carried on. He saw that in spite of everything the crowds were still listening. His voice was strong.

'Jesus said, "Lo I am with you always, you who preach forgiveness of sins in my name even unto the end of the world." When the gospel of Christ is preached his kingdom is not far from any of you. You may enter into it, if you listen to his voice. Repent and listen to his voice. Repent and believe the gospel.'

Sarah heard all this. The stones still flew. Then she saw her curate Kitson lounging against the platform and smiling, encouraging the stone throwers in front of her. Her fury rose. She stormed through the crowd to him.

'Why don't you stop them?' she shouted.

Curate Kitson bowed to her. 'This is not the place for you, Miss Crossman. Go back home. I warned that fellow not to preach here, but he was too damned pig-headed to take my advice.'

The stones still flew, but so did John Wesley's words.

'They're running out of stones,' gasped Sophia in a mixture

of fear and excitement, as she and Mrs Collington joined Sarah.

'Stop, the scoundrel who knocks down our churches,' shouted one voice repetitively.

'Beg for mercy, you damned Methodist,' shouted the leader of the gang in front of Sarah.

He pushed his way towards the front of the platform and threw his last stone from less than a few metres. It hit John Wesley's face, and blood covered his forehead.

'Down with dissenters,' yelled the ruffian, and then sensing that he had earned his reward and that those around him were not on his side, he disappeared from the scene.

John Wesley fell forward on his knees, clasping his head. Sarah, Mrs Collington and Sophia clambered on to the platform and Sarah was soon kneeling beside him. She offered him a kerchief, which he received with thanks and wiped away the blood.

'God has given to them who believe not the spirit of fear, but of power and of love and of a sound mind.'

His friends ushered him off the stage.

'I am not hurt,' he said to Sarah with a smile. Farmer Walter's cows were still mooing on the far side of the garden.

'Many of the beasts of the people laboured much to disturb those who were of a better mind. They tried to drive us out with cows, but the brutes were wiser than their masters.'

With a bow, he repeated his thanks to Sarah, and wished that they might meet again.

Sarah, Mrs Collington and Sophia returned home happy on that lovely September afternoon.

16

Richard walked over to the white man. He was clearly ill and not dangerous. Even if he rose from his bed he could not walk fast with the chains gripping his ankles. He picked up a dirty metal bowl. The white man opened his eyes.

'Water,' he gasped.

Richard did not reply. He walked confidently outside and Selina joined him as he knelt by the river and filled the bowl with brown river water.

'Let the mud sink to the bottom,' suggested Selina.

'He's Mr Clow's assistant. Father has talked about him. I am going to help him.'

They went back together. The white man propped himself on one shoulder. His whole body was shaking. He lay back on the wooden pillow and stretched out his hands to Richard. He took the bowl and started to drink. The water splashed over his face and shirt, but some went down his throat.

'More,' he spluttered.

Richard took the bowl and went back to the river.

Selina stared at the white man. The white man stared at Selina.

'Polly,' he said.

'My name is Selina,' she replied. 'Not Polly.'

'I love Polly, Polly Catlett, but I shall not see her again,' the white man muttered as if to himself. 'Murdered by a treacherous, filthy, evil black creature . . . .'

'What is your name?' asked Selina firmly.

The white man looked at her. His whole body shuddered.

'John Newton,' he muttered.

Richard returned with more muddy water. Trembling hands grabbed it.

'He's called John Newton,' said Selina.

'You work for Mr Clow?' asked Richard.

'I did till he sailed away, and now I am a slave of slaves. Because I have a fever this damned princess made me a slave. She hopes that I shall die. She feeds me with the foul scraps from her plate, scraps her own teeth have chewed, and rice the slaves have brushed up from under her table. Even her slaves have kinder hearts but they dare not cross her will.'

Richard was horrified.

'We will rescue you.'

For the first time a faint smile crossed his weary, fever ridden face.

'No, no, but you can help. Where do you live?'

'At the mouth of the Camaranca.'

'Tell your father about me. I could work for him.' His eyes turned wild again. 'Food, bring me food. I begged her when she came to laugh at me for food. She told me to call her the Princess of the Plantains and to bow before her. I thought I could not do such a shameful thing, but I did. She laughed and went away. Then she came back and with scorn she handed me a plate with a half-eaten fish, and a pile of dirty rice. How I longed to eat it. Here was a feast indeed. She made me stretch my arms to reach it. My fingers were too weak to hold it. It fell to the ground. You who live in plenty can hardly conceive how this loss touched me, but the princess knew and had the cruelty to laugh at my disappointment. She would not let me kneel to take it off the ground, nor would she give me any more. When I tried to get it she called me "worthless" and "lazy" and said she would have me whipped like her other slaves. I was dragged back to this log.'

The effort of fluent talking made him flop back again.

'Food, food. Polly Catlett, Polly . . . .'

Then the fever took over and made him inaudible though he went on muttering and swearing.

Richard led the fascinated Selina out of the hut.

The thoughts of the boy were on the horror of a black woman having a white man whipped; the thoughts of Selina were on Polly not knowing of the fate of the man she hoped to marry.

17

Sarah wrote a long letter to her brother-in-law, Sir Adam in December 1742. In it she wished Sir Adam, her sister, Katharine, and her nephew, George, Christmas greetings. Then she wrote a long and vivid account of her visit to the Great Gardens in Whitechapel. Lady Katharine was amused.

'They had a most fortunate escape,' she said to her husband.

'I think, Lady Katharine,' replied Sir Adam in what he felt were wise, measured words, 'that though I am as relieved as you are that no ill befell Sarah, there is a certain, a certain, how shall I say it, a certain trend, no, better than that, a certain drift which suggests Sarah may end wrecked on a rocky coast.' Sir Adam was pleased with his speech, but he noted Lady Katharine was gazing at him in some blankness. 'If you follow me, my dear,' he added.

'I didn't remember Sarah saying anything about going to sea,' she replied.

Sir Adam was as baffled with his wife's reply as she had been with his.

'Sarah seems to be praising this charlatan John Wesley. I have heard from Parson Blackman that he stirs up riots, robs widows of their savings, and encourages love-feasts with his followers. I would rather not say what happens when they put the candles out at these gatherings.'

'It hardly seems to be the same man. However I think there is little cause for alarm with Sarah. She merely said she liked the man more than the mob who attacked him. She is very orthodox in her beliefs, is regularly at church, and often at the sacrament.'

'Her own goodness may prevent her from recognizing a wolf in sheep's clothing. I shall write to John Blackman at once. There would be no-one better to warn and reprimand her.

And, Lady Katharine, a little bird has told me John would welcome a journey out to Whitechapel to visit Sarah.'

Sir Adam composed his reply to his friend, the Rector of Barcombe.

18

Richard and Selina knew they should find their father. Richard was fancying rescuing John Newton from that 'damned she-devil'. However the heroic deeds he was planning were forgotten for as they walked along the river bank they heard their father's voice. They trotted past a hut and saw him standing by their boat.

'Shall we tell him?' asked Selina.

'Leave that to me,' replied the masterful Richard.

Henry Calvert was glad to see them safe. His talk with the princess had left him uneasy and upset. The sight of his two children was reassuring. He realized he loved them and he also realized it was the first time he had ever consciously thought that. He found it hard to express his feelings and indeed as they ran up he said crossly, 'Where have you been? I have been waiting.'

'She wouldn't let us in,' complained Richard, avoiding the question. 'A slave stopped us.'

'I don't like the princess,' said Selina.

'She is watching us,' said Richard as their slave was pushing the boat away with the oar.

They all looked back at the house, and there was the clear shadow of the princess at the window. The Calverts couldn't see her expression, and this was just as well. Scorn and hate filled the princess's face.

Her scorn was for all white people; even her husband was included though to a lesser degree. She decided that whites were feeble even in their dishonesty and greed. The hate arose from them being successful rivals. Her conversation with Henry Calvert confirmed what she already thought. There was no room for both the Calverts and the Clows. The Calverts must go. The princess knew that without any Western education she could outwit any white man in cunning and perseverance.

The loss of the two children in the river would surely have sent their parents away broken-hearted. She watched as the slaves rowed Richard and Selina away safe. Her face showed no disappointment. Other plans were already in her mind. As she had promised she was preparing a message for King Ambo.

19

The Reverend John Blackman, rector of Barcombe and many other places was not displeased to receive Sir Adam's letter. A visit to Whitechapel would take him from the comfortable life of drinking, gambling and fellowship with old friends at the Cocoa Tree. He did not enjoy visiting parishioners, but it was different with Sarah.

If he were ever to stray from being a bachelor it would be Sarah who received the honour of his proposal. Her beauty and wit were enhanced by her income of two thousand pounds a year and her fine house.

At times her presence carried him away. Once while staying with her at Kilmore House, he had slightly altered one of Pope's poems.

'I know a thing that's most uncommon,
(Sarah, be silent and attend!)
I know a reasonable woman,
Handsome and witty, yet a friend.'

His passion however cooled before he sent it. Her virtues had to be considered carefully and balanced with his love of life at the Cocoa Tree. He had placed the paper carefully in his Prayer Book for further consideration. He re-read the poem. Yes, reasonable woman. That was the key to it. Life must be ruled by reason. And was Sarah reasonable?

He had dined well on goose-pie covered with the sauce the Cocoa Tree was famous for. He watched his card playing friends as he sipped his whisky punch. No, no handsome, witty Sarah would take him from these delights. But he would do as Sir Adam asked and he looked forward to the visit.

He summoned a servant and asked for writing paper.

20

The Calverts' journey home was silent. They all had much to think about.

Henry was pondering his visit to King Ambo, who had a great reputation as a collector of slaves. He had soldiers that were feared. Slave-trading had brought continual fighting to the Guinea coast. Henry had seen on his trips up river that as soon as the rains were over and the harvest gathered in, King Ambo and other powerful chiefs set about harvesting their other main crop, slaves. The soldiers raided villages around. They seized all the men, women and children they could, chased and caught most of those who fled into the jungle, rounded up the cattle and then set fire to the village. It was then that a slave-trader would appear and bargain for the slaves. A long, sad, chained coffle would then be led to the coast. This was Henry's business.

However the princess had surprised him. If she knew King Ambo as she probably did, why was she not bargaining for slaves herself. Henry knew that Sebastian had not had a good season. He suspected that this failure had led Sebastian to get married to this extraordinary woman.

He then considered her advice, almost a warning, not to barter with guns. Henry appreciated the sense of this, for if powerful men like Ambo had well-armed soldiers, the slave-trader's factories might be in danger. Their white authority and the threat of the British navy could be a crumbling wall against an ambitious Ambo. Yet guns and gunpowder were easily Henry's most valuable swapping goods.

Slaves were bartered for in 'bars'. Forty years earlier these had been bars of iron, but now they were the currency used for slave-trading. Henry valued a gallon of brandy at three bars, a length of cloth at eight, a solid kettle at four, but one gun with gunpowder might reach fifteen bars. Women and children could be bought for four to ten bars. Henry decided to discuss it with Sebastian later.

46

Richard thought hard about John Newton and his chains. At last he said, 'Father, there is a white man in a slave hut by the river.'

'What?' Henry recalled his thoughts. 'White man? Where?'

'In the Clow's slave hut.'

'A white man? Sebastian is away.'

'Not Mr Clow. It's John Newton. He's lying on a box.'

'He's very ill,' added Selina.

'His ankles are chained together like a slave.'

'I think he is starving.'

'A white man with chains on?' Henry was baffled. 'Wait, I believe Sebastian was taking on a young, white assistant. I thought he was going north with him up to the Portuguese factories.'

'He didn't look like an assistant. He looked like a slave,' Richard said.

'He hates the princess,' put in Selina. 'And he swore.'

'Well, it is not our business,' said Henry. 'Sebastian will tell me about it later. Perhaps this John Newton has turned out to be a scoundrel.'

'We ought to take him some food,' said Selina.

'Be silent,' retorted her father sharply. He did not take kindly to his daughter contradicting him. 'You speak of things that do not concern you.'

There was silence as they disembarked.

Henry walked ahead. Selina said quietly to Richard, 'I'm going to take him some food.'

21

Sophia showed the Reverend John Blackman into her mistress's drawing room, stepping smartly aside at the last moment to avoid having her bottom pinched. She knew this gentleman well from times when she was with her mistress at Kilmore House.

'He's a jolly gentleman,' she used to say.

'Mr Blackman,' she announced.

Sarah rose and offered him a hand to kiss and a chair.

John was pleased to note that she was as pretty and clean and unperfumed as ever.

'To what do I owe the honour of this visit, John? Is it to tell me of some new places of which you are rector or has the court offered you a bishopric at last?'

John was happy. Only Sarah would speak frankly to him like this. What is more it would lead gently into the purpose of his visit. Even as a child Sarah had not taken kindly to admonishments.

'No, my dear Sarah. I have enough parishes to provide me with the income I require, and no bishoprics will come to me from the Whigs. I trust I am not a greedy man.'

'I think there are some of your parishes that you have never visited,' remarked Sarah in such a way that it was a question.

John was slightly worried. Was she influenced by this ruffian Wesley?

'Ah, you always had a satirical wit, Sarah. You do not understand the business of life. And, indeed, why should you? I have been to nearly all my parishes, all except that one far away in Warwickshire. I go regularly to the others to negotiate the tithes and to make sure they are paid. There are, I fear, many who try to avoid paying their dues to the church.'

'That is what I said,' replied Sarah. 'You go to see your parishioners to get money from them and not to look after them.'

The cool Mr Blackman felt slightly warmer.

'I send each parish a curate who costs me forty pounds. He preaches, and looks after the poor.'

'Parson Chipperfield doesn't preach at Barcombe if it is raining, I was once told.'

'If the Bishop is dissatisfied, Parson Chipperfield will be rebuked. But that is not my responsibility. My friend, the Bishop of Llandaff, has praised me for my moderation in accepting livings.'

Sarah laughed.

'You've told me about Bishop Watson before. You said he had, apart from his diocese, two parishes in Shropshire, two in Leicestershire, two in the Isle of Ely and many others.'

John wished they had not had a good laugh over Bishop Watson.

'And you said,' pursued Sarah, 'that he didn't live in any of them. He had a farm in Westmorland. You read a letter from him in which he thought that the improvement of a man's fortune was the most useful and honourable way of providing for a family.'

'Tell me, Sarah,' interrupted John, 'where are you getting these ideas from?'

'My ideas have always come from me,' replied Sarah confidently.

John reflected that there was a certain truth in this. He could remember occasions in Whitechapel and at Kilmore House when all the combined forces of church and nobility had been thwarted by Sarah.

'But I gather from Sir Adam that you have been talking to that trouble-maker, Wesley?'

Sarah's eyes glistened with delight. It was as she thought. John was her to prevent her going astray. Sarah loved others thinking she was going astray.

'I may have chatted with that person once or twice. He caused no trouble. In fact he suffered from trouble caused by others including our curate at Whitechapel.'

'Now, my dear Sarah,' said John changing the conversation. 'You must listen to me as your Rector and as an older man who has seen many things you have not, and who has the ear of ministers and bishops.' He looked at Sarah with some anxiety, but she sat upright, innocently quiet.

'We have had wars in the past over religion. Now we have a calmer creed and common sense. The church has the duty to tell the common people to ignore the enthusiast, who encourages mobs. We all must behave according to reason. Now this firebrand, Wesley, makes people go mad with his words. This is not reason. He raises mobs . . . .'

'It is not Wesley who raised the mob here,' interrupted Sarah. 'It was Curate Kitson.'

'You always complain, Sarah, that your Curate at Whitechapel is dry as dust, and dull and mean. If, as you believe, he raised a mob and paid for it to thwart this Wesley man, then all your accusations are false.'

Sarah laughed, though she also appreciated that her point had not been answered.

'You may be right, most holy John,' she retorted, 'but be assured I shall take the words of Wesley no more seriously than I do the words of my Rector. Now, no more theology. I shall ring for tea.'

With that John had to be satisfied. He enjoyed his visit. He pondered again as a sedan chair carried him back to the Cocoa Tree Club about the loneliness of life as a bachelor compared with the companionship of someone like Sarah with her sparkling beauty and inclination to argue.

22

Peggy Calvert never knew the full story of her husband's and children's visit. She knew nothing of the children's near death in the river, and the princess's part in it, and little of the assistant, the ill and unhappy John Newton. However she was most interested in Henry's meeting with the princess. In her heart she recognized a worthy rival. With the Plantains Factory as close as it was to Camaranca there never had been as many slaves as they both wanted but Henry and Sebastian Clow had worked together in reasonable harmony. Indeed, Henry had been more successful than Sebastian, who clearly had rushed into marriage to improve his prospects.

She was puzzled over Mrs Clow's (she insisted on calling her this) encouragement of the visit to King Ambo. For a long time they had planned this trip up the Camaranca river. Ambo was known as the most successful, ruthless and belligerent of the inland chiefs. The more war-like and ruthless the chiefs were, the more slaves they had, but these qualities also meant the more dangerous they were.

In the past if a white trader had been killed by the natives, the Royal Navy had always been called in and provided rough justice. But Ambo was many miles up river, and therefore safe from naval expeditions.

Clearly Ambo without guns was preferable to Ambo with them, but Peggy was a born trader and realized as Henry had done, that what was desirable might well not be attainable. Nevertheless, Mrs Clow's advice might be a good starting point for discussions with Ambo over the price of his slaves.

Peggy reckoned that the expedition was worth undertaking. Henry was good at drawing trust from even difficult chiefs. She urged him to go, but her husband hesitated, and said he would have a talk with Sebastian before he journeyed up river.

When news came that Sebastian had returned from his

expedition, Henry was being rowed over to see him. Richard and Selina were there too. Henry was quietly glad of their enthusiasm to go with him and learn their trade. Selina was clutching, as unobtrusively as possible, something wrapped in banana leaves.

23

In the following months, Sarah Crossman met Mr Wesley several times after she had heard him in the Great Gardens. He puzzled her. She had admired his courage, and his humour ('the beasts of the field show more wisdom that the beast of men,' he had said as she bathed his wounded brow).

It was his beliefs that puzzled her most. She had listened to sermons all her life. Providence was the power which bestows its favour or otherwise, which made you rich or poor and which, if tried, would give you happiness in heaven. Many sermons had urged her to do duties suitable to the light of nature, to keep a good reputation, and to live to the best reason of mankind. To Sarah it had seemed often dull, often vague but on the whole sensible.

She then explained how she earned her money, Wesley did not approve. Sarah who had never seen a slave, explained the advantages they gained after being captured by white men.

'All men are created equal in God's sight,' said Wesley.

'But these are not men in that sense,' replied Sarah, 'they are black, and have not the same power as we have.'

'In what do you put your faith? In the power of reason?' asked John.

'Yes, and in the power of the church which had moulded the reason of all ages and of many people into an understandable religion. Is not that your faith too? You are a parson.'

'My faith is in a person. I believe that through the merits of Jesus Christ, my sins are forgiven and I am reconciled in favour of God.'

Sarah did not understand this, though when she thought about it later and remembered the phrases from the communion service mumbled through every month in church, her mind began to clear. She had more questions for John Blackman.

She had finished her third meeting with Mr Wesley by

inviting him to Kilmore House. Sir Adam could not refuse a guest of hers.

Wesley smiled.

'It may be possible one day, but the men of Sussex love smugglers; they do not want to love the Lord Jesus Christ.'

Thus her visit to Kilmore House that year in 1744 included only one John, the Rector of Barcombe. Her discussions with Wesley gained her he reputation of being religious. John was a peace-loving man as well as a clever one and did not condemn her. Sir Adam was neither so kind nor so clever but did not condemn her either for she was generous to the Kilmores. Nevertheless, he worried. Enthusiasm in religion was the first sign of madness to Sir Adam, and a putting of emotion above reason was an equally dangerous disease.

Lady Katharine was not so worried about any religious feelings, but more about Sarah's views on slaves. It was from Sarah's slave-trading money that Katharine often helped Sir Adam in the expenses of Kilmore House. Sarah had read Daniel Defoe's *Robinson Crusoe* and had said it was against slave-trading. Her sister who had not read a book for twenty-five years started to read it, so that she could refute Sarah.

Sir Adam, however, was growing less interested about Sarah and her views, and more interested in his safety and his reputation. His garden house was filled with large packs of tea. Every one of his gardeners knew, and though to a Sussex man smuggling was as natural as drinking, Sir Adam realized that while his income was safer than it had ever been, his reputation was not. A large proclamation had appeared in Lewes, in which His Majesty offered pardon to any smuggler who gave information about other smugglers, and a large reward as well. Sir Adam wondered whether he should increase the wages of his young gardeners to eight shillings a week.

24

The Calvert family stepped ashore at the Plantains and Henry was glad to see Sebastian Clow coming down to meet them. They greeted one another and slowly strolled towards the house. The children were ignored. They watched their father disappear into the house. They could see no sign of the princess.

'Come on,' said Selina pulling at Richard's arm. 'We must find John Newton.'

They ran along the riverbank to the hut. It was empty.

'Perhaps he is working for Mr Clow.'

'Perhaps he has escaped.'

'Or is dead.'

'Oh no, come on, let us go to the kitchen and ask where he is,' said Selina bravely.

Richard hesitated. They were doing all the things they should not, but he wanted to find John Newton too. They made their way cautiously to the kitchen keeping other buildings between them and the house. The thought of the princess watching them made them shiver.

One female slave was working at a table cutting up chickens. She looked frightened as they stood in the doorway.

'Where is John Newton?' Richard asked boldly.

The slave did not reply, but looked towards the house with worried eyes.

'We will not tell anyone what you say. Is he dead?' asked Selina.

Again she was silent, and then shook her head.

'He is not in the hut,' said Richard. 'Where is he?'

She pointed her hand away from the river and to the land behind the house.

'He work,' she muttered, and then returned to her cooking and ignored them.

'Come on,' said Richard. 'We shall have a look. He must be making the slaves work in the garden.'

'Let us keep behind the trees. I don't want anyone to see us.' They left the kitchen and using the banana trees as shelter worked their way behind the house into what clearly was being changed into a garden from the jungle that covered the centre of the island.

'He's there,' gasped Selina pointing across the garden.

'Back behind the trees,' said Richard grabbing her. 'Let us see what is happening.'

He still has the chains on his legs. He's working with a black slave.'

They gazed in astonishment. The native was loosening the ground with a long-handled axe, and John Newton was planting small trees behind him. He was nearly naked like the slave.

'He can hardly walk,' said Richard. 'He still has the fever. We must help him. Follow me, Selina. Keep behind the trees and out of sight of the house.'

They worked their way round the semi-circle of trees, and had nearly reached them when Richard grabbed Selina's arm and pulled her down behind a large tree. They crouched and looked. Neither the white nor the black slave had noticed them. They worked with downcast, hapless eyes.

'The princess,' hissed Richard.

From the house stepped the Princess with a slave escort behind.

25

It was dark. Sir Adam watched as six wagons rumbled past his study, round the kitchens and into the gardens stretching down to the Ouse. By the light of lanterns he recognized the faces of Barcombe men who worked in the fields by day and had other occupations by night. He saw the lined, weather-beaten weary faces of Hugh Lines, Edmund Anscombe, Daniel Bull, Robert Lockwood, Arthur Scott, Philip Cottingham, George Harding, Jonathan Hindley, Ebenezer Collard, John Waters and Thomas Willis. Cloth hats were pulled over their heads and in their belts under their short coats a short cudgel was ready by their right hand.

Sir Adam was glad that his wife was away at Whitechapel, George was in bed asleep, and those servants who were in the house were, at his command, turning their eyes away. The men who led the horses were best forgotten.

The wagons rumbled to a halt by the garden house. Sir Adam saw shadows pass to and fro in front of the lanterns, but he heard not a sound.

In half an hour the horses dragged the wagons past the house and out into the Sussex lanes.

The garden house was empty.

26

Richard and Selina saw the princess stalk towards John Newton. A smile crossed her face. She beckoned her slave to her side, pointed at John and started to scream at him. Though her language was still halting, Englishmen she had met had already taught her how to swear.

John did not look at her or seem to hear her. Awkwardly he bent down and pushed another little lime tree into the ground.

The princess began to imitate his clumsy movements, and, speaking in her own tongue to her escort, encouraged her to mimic him too. They laughed and clapped their hands together in a dance. Then the princess picked up a stone and threw it at him. Her escort did the same. Some stones hit John. He shielded his face but said nothing. Then they tired of this and wandered back to the house still laughing.

Richard could hardly believe his eyes. He wanted to run to help John, but common sense held him back. The princess went inside. For ten seconds they gazed at the door; then clutching hands they galloped over the ground to John who was kneeling by a pile of lime tree shoots staring at the ground.

'John Newton,' called Selina, 'I've food for you.'

She thrust her little bundle on to the earth in front of him. Out fell wings and legs of chicken, cooked fish, bread and bananas.

A quick smile crossed John's bleeding face. Then it passed.

'I am a servant of slaves,' he muttered.

He seized the chicken leg and gnawed at it still on his knees. Then he signalled to his silent black companion, who came over. John handed some chicken to him.

'Black slaves feed me; not that damned princess.'

Then he was silent, listening. They all listened. Men's voices drifted from the house.

'Take the food. Hide it in the hut under the book. Take the

letter from the book. Send it to England.' He stood up and looked at the children. Tears came into his eyes. He bent down, picked up Selina, and kissed her. He lowered gently and sobbed as he muttered, 'the hut, the hut and ... .' They couldn't hear any more.

The children bent low and ran back into the shade of the trees. In their safe shade Selina looked back at John.

'He kissed me,' she said in delight.

'It's our father,' Richard whispered. Coming out of the house were their father, Mr Clow with the black princess on his arm, and her attendant behind. They strolled over to where John Newton was working. He staggered partly from his chains and partly from weakness as he returned to the spot where he had been planting with a fresh set of little limes.

The children heard Mr Clow talking to their father, but only heard the word "punishment". Then Mr Clow turned to John and said loudly and in fun, 'Who knows but by the time these trees grow up and bear, you may go home to England, obtain the command of a ship and return to reap the fruits of your labours? We see strange things happen sometimes.'

Mr Clow and his wife roared with laughter and turned towards the house. Their father did not laugh but walked along with them.

'We must do what John says,' said Richard. 'Come on, hurry, Selina. Father will be back at the boat soon.'

They ran through the plantains back to the hut. It was still empty. they soon saw the book lying on the ground by his bed. Richard picked it up. He was a good reader, but he had some difficulty with its title.

'It's ... it's Euclid's *Elements of Geometry*.'

'Geometry, what's that?' asked Selina.

Richard opened the book and they gazed at pictures of triangles.

'Look,' said Selina, 'there are some of those over here on the ground.'

On the other side of the bed Selina had noticed lines drawn in the sand with a stick. Richard looked at them.

'They are triangles,' he said authoritatively.

'I'm going to bury the food.'

Selina kicked away a hole in the sandy floor and was just about to push the food wrapped in plantain leaves into it, when she remembered something.

'A letter? What did John say about a letter?'

Richard had been reading the book with some interest.

'Oh yes, letter in the book.'

He shook the tattered brown book. Out fell the folded sheet of paper addressed to Captain Joseph Manesty, Liverpool for Captain John Newton.

Selina was disappointed. She had hoped for a letter to Polly.

'We will put it in our father's mailbag,' said Richard. 'No-one will know.' He covered the food with earth again as Selina looked at the book. 'There's another letter in it stuck at the back.' She pulled it out.

'It's to Polly Catlett at Chatham.' read Richard.

'A love letter! We will send this too,' added his sister.

'Put the book on the ground here,' ordered Richard. 'Now we must hurry back to the boat.'

To their relief they found themselves back at the boat with the four patient slaves before their father arrived.

27

Giving parties at Kilmore House was one of the joys of Lady Katharine's life, and what now was more fashionable than a tea party? All the important ladies and gentlemen of Ringmer, Chailey, Newick, Lewes and Barcombe were there. So too were Sarah, the Rector of Barcombe, John Blackman, and his curate, Eugene Chipperfield.

In front of a blazing log fire, Sir Roger King, the squire of Ringmer talked with casual superiority of his friendship with his neighbour, the Duke of Newcastle, at Laughton.

'Mark my words, Medley,' he said to the Lord of the Manor at Barcombe, 'when the Duke wishes to hear how the gentlemen of England feel, it is to the squire of Ringmer he comes. Is that not true, Marsh?' he asked, moving forward from the fire as the trousers of one gentleman of England felt too warm.

Sir Charles agreed and mentioned Newcastle's help over free-trading. Sir Adam's pride at the gathering was equal to that of his wife, but as Sir Roger's voice boomed about free-trading above the crackling fire, he felt obliged to usher Captain Matthew Kay to the far side of the room.

'What could have got into Sir Roger,' he thought, 'to bring this dangerous young officer from the dragoons? And then to talk about free-trading!'

'He will be the next Prime Minister,' announced Sir Roger.

'He has not been much of a success as Defence Minister,' replied Sir Charles, who could not bear any boasting from others, 'unless losing all our friends abroad means that now we are in greater need of a Defence Minister.'

All the gentlemen laughed except Sir Roger.

Lady Katharine glowed with pride as she half heard this conversation. The beauty of ladies' clothes (though none more beautiful than hers as Sir Charles had said), the handsome, important men in their finest wigs, the buzz of conversation and the satisfying, wafted smell of the tea made her so thankful that she lived in this enlightened age.

'My dragoons,' complained Captain Kay, 'hate this service in Sussex looking for smugglers. They are tired and wet and nobody welcomes them. They would rather be fighting the French than floundering along muddy paths, lying behind gorse bushes on the downs, being whipped by branches in the woods and finding no-one. I tell them they get good pay of two pennies a day and they are still alive. And still they grumble.'

'I do not put up with grumbling in Ringmer. The whole village comes to church at my command, and if anyone has caused trouble I go over and make them stand up and apologize,' replied the rotund and rosy Sir Roger.

'Does not the parson object?' asked Captain Kay.

'Parsons are not here to object. They are here to serve their superiors.'

'You mean God,' said Sarah sweetly.

'God? No, not God,' replied Sir Roger crossly, turning to face Sarah. Then as he found she was pretty, he went on in a kinder tone. 'I mean the squire, the gentleman whom God has put in charge.'

He was pleased with this reply.

Sir Charles Marsh interrupted.

'Your dragoons waste their time here, Captain. They should be at Rye. That is where smugglers flourish, I am told.'

Parson Eugene Chipperfield was trying to corner his Rector but his eyes were fixed on Sarah across the room.

'I have worked faithfully for four years in your parish,' pleaded the Curate, 'but it is hard to clothe and feed my wife, my children and my servant on that money.'

'You have my grand rectory,' said John.

Eugene was just about to explain the damp and the cold when the Rector said, 'We must talk about it further,' and without any such intention he moved across the room towards Sarah.

'I scorn to patch and paint myself,' said young Lady Ruth King to a lady who clearly did not scorn to do so.

'If God has given me beauty it would indeed be ungrateful of me not to labour to improve it,' came the chilling reply.

'For a time I was suspicious of Jebb at the Sloop Inn. There seemed much trade up and down the river by day and night.

62

But I have found him to be a generous man to me and my dragoons. Now I feel as comfortable there as I do at home,' said Captain Kay.

'More so, perhaps,' commented Sir Charles amid laughter. 'I doubt whether Mrs Kay can provide such a steady river of brandy.'

'As long as the river of brandy has not come up the River Ouse,' replied the Captain.

Sir Adam gave a start when he heard this. But everyone else roared with laughter and he realized gratefully that the Captain had been making a joke.

The Rector had cornered Sarah, and as ever she was being awkward.

'You must recognize, my dear Sarah that negroes are a degenerate race with a feeble sense of what is right and wrong. They are not men in the way these gentlemen are. We trade with cattle and we trade with slaves. Indeed they profit from our labours. I am told that these poor benighted black wretches in Africa, if they were suspected of a small degree of crime, would suffer from the butcher's knife of the tribal chief in their own village.'

'You speak about what you hear, John, not about what you have seen,' argued Sarah. 'Robinson Crusoe said he could not do cruel things to innocent natives who had done him no harm, and had helped him.'

'I doubt whether Defoe ever met one of these innocent creatures.'

Sarah was not to be deflected easily.

'John Wesley says,' she began.

'Ah, I hear that beguiling name again. No more . . .' but he was interrupted by the call of his host.

'Come gentlemen, to my study. I have another liquid there with which to drink the health of our Captain.'

The men trooped off.

As they drank with self-satisfied jollity, Sir Adam felt happier than he had for some time. He looked forward to future profits. A coming load for the garden house now tossing on the channel was merely part of the card game in which he was going to hold the trumps. The Captain is one of us, he thought.

The house of Kilmore will prosper again. He planned to have his crest and motto carved in stone and placed above his front door. He had noticed Sir Roger had done this at Newick. Sir Adam's motto was *Pensez à Moi*.

28

'Sebastian is a changed man,' reported Henry Calvert to his wife.

'That usually happens in marriage, and it's nearly always for the better,' replied his wife drily. 'What did he say about Ambo?'

'He agrees with the princess. He has learnt much about Ambo from her, and it seems he is powerful in gold, ivory and slaves. He wants guns in particular, but the princess fears that if he gained enough he would move down river and that would be the end of the Clows and us.'

'I must meet this Mrs Clow,' said Peggy. 'She has more sense that I could have expected. There is one point that surprises me. Why does not Sebastian go if her knowledge of Ambo is so great. I suspect she does not wish us well.'

'Indeed, Peggy, I too considered that. It seems that though the princess's father and Ambo were once friends, they have recently quarrelled when they were both interested in gaining slaves from the same villages. Thus Mr Clow would not be welcome since his marriage.'

'Even so; why does Mrs Clow encourage us?'

'There may be a reason that arises less from charity and more from prudence,' replied Henry. 'Sebastian suggested I think that were we successful we might in gratitude pass on some of the slaves to him.'

'That is the best news you have given me, Henry. I am suspicious of charity, the more so from a black. But this is a business venture. You shall visit Ambo. Whether the Clows will gain from it we shall see.'

29

Katharine and Sarah sat together after the party. There was much to discuss; they had to pass on the gossip they had heard.

Sarah soon sensed that Katharine's happiness over the party's success was fading. From old she knew when her sister was worried. She tried to find out why. No, it was not George, or the servants or Peggy and her children in Sierra Leone.

'I trust that the Kilmore business prospers.' Sarah, at once saw she had made a hit. Katharine blushed and looked away.

'What troubles you, Cat?' asked Sarah, using her sister's nickname again after twenty years.

Katharine looked up.

'I have a confession, Sarah. It must remain with you.'

'It shall,' replied her sister.

'I was in Sir Adam's study a week ago, and a gust of wind blew some papers from his desk. I picked them up, but I couldn't help noticing that one of them was about the Kilmore Trading Company. I read it casually till I found it was an account of two dreadful disasters which had left the company with nothing but debts. Two of his captains left Africa with good cargoes of slaves. One was drunk it seems, for most of the voyage. He lost control of his crew who stole the brandy, killed some of the slaves and threw others who rebelled overboard. Of the two hundred slaves only five could be sold in Antigua. On the next ship the captain said the slaves refused to eat. Many died in their chains and those who could go ashore were too weak and their price was pitifully low. Each ship should have made a profit of £700. They made nothing.'

'But Peggy and I can help you, Cat,' comforted Sarah. 'I know Peggy has been sending you money for Richard.'

'It's not that. Sir Adam now has plenty of money. I saw some being delivered yesterday. Sir Adam took a bag full of coins from someone who is no gentleman, and hid them from me. And . . . and . . . when later I went to look there was a good three hundred pounds there.'

'He's been betting. Lord Montford told me that there were three actions that characterize a gentleman. It is not proper to mention one of them but the other two were drinking brandy and having a daily bet. Adam drinks brandy and perhaps he has his daily bet. That is where his money comes from.'

'I wish it did, Sarah. I fear you are wrong.'

30

There was great excitement for Richard and Selina at Camaranca. They were going with their father to visit King Ambo. Their mother had intended to keep them at home for lessons, but was suffering greatly from fever.

Richard and Selina had watched the sad lines of slaves being brought from the huts. The slave ship *Halifax* was a mile off shore almost ready for the Middle Passage to the West Indies. The Captain and his Mate were talking with Henry Calvert. A rough band of sailors stood by, some holding whips, and some light chains with clamps on the end.

The Calvert's house-servants brought the slaves forward one by one for inspection. The slaves were naked and fearful. If the Captain saw any defect in them he turned them away and they were led back to be chained again in the hut. Over some of them there was bargaining between the Captain and Henry, but Henry was clearly pleased. The Captain was anxious to fill his ship and get away. He took most of the slaves, paying twelve pounds for the best, and four pounds for some boys and girls who were no older than Richard and Selina.

One small boy cried with alarm and ran away after his mother who had been turned back as unfit for the voyage. A sailor chased after him with a whip and lashed him as he fled into the trees. The boy fell and was roughly dragged back, chained, pushed before the Captain and passed for the voyage.

'I do not like it,' said Richard.

'He should stay with his mother,' said Selina.

'Come on. We will not stay here,' said Richard and, as they watched the little slave forced towards the canoe waiting to take them to the *Halifax*, the sailor whipped him on.

They went inside to their mother, lying on her bed.

'The sailors are brutes,' said Richard.

'They won't let a boy go with his mother,' cried Selina. 'And they keep on beating him.'

'They are all going to a better land,' replied their mother. 'They do not feel pain like white people do. Your father says the Captain is paying a good price. Now, go down to the stores and tell Sam to carry the goods to the shallop. You can help him.'

31

The Reverend John Blackman had been rector of Barcombe since 1709 in the reign of Good Queen Anne. He was pleased with this position. His salary of four hundred pounds a year and a good rectory near the church of St Mary the Virgin, had been the basis of a happy life in London. He had always been faithful in his supply of a curate to help the poor in the parish. Parson Chipperfield who enjoyed the rectory might be selfish in continually demanding more than his already generous forty pounds, but he was a useful tutor for George. It was to the rich in Barcombe that John felt called. Indeed he quoted from the Bible that it was hard for the rich to enter the kingdom of heaven. Thus he had chosen the harder task.

He was not ambitious. Indeed to be a bishop he must first become a Whig. His acquaintance, the Reverend James Baker became an enthusiastic Whig and the election agent of the Duke of Newcastle (he had more power in choice of new bishops than the Archbishop of Canterbury). Once when James Baker had wished to make a speech for the Duke he had interrupted a game of cricket at Lewes. He was nearly mobbed by the spectators. The cricket match went on.

John was like Sir Adam, a Jacobite at heart, and made many witty comments on the German king, but it was pleasure not politics that interested him.

Religion had come through the dark ages of strife to the age of order, reason and happiness. The fear of eternal punishment had been dismissed by the bishops. John had no time for emotion ('a flight from reason') or personal responsibility ('wildfire from Wesley') but rather that we should follow a sensible moral life, which led to happiness in this life and doubtless in the next too.

But though he kept emotion out of religion he could not altogether keep it out of his life, especially when he was in the same house as Sarah.

And here he was in Kilmore House. And so was Sarah and Sarah had asked to see him privately that evening. He walked to the window and looked out over the field that stretched down to the meandering Ouse. Beyond lay the South Downs, on which the sun was setting. Above a new moon and some bold stars shone. Emotion crept in. He was moved by the sight.

The poet Addison had it right.

> 'What though in solemn silence all
> Move round the dark celestial ball;
> What though no real voice or sound
> Amidst their radiant orbs be found;
> In reason's ear they all rejoice,
> And utter forth a glorious voice,
> For ever singing, as they shine,
> "The hand that made us is divine".'

Yes; there was indeed no real voice, but the beauty of nature and reason still spoke of God.

Then there was a knock, and a real voice. And there was beauty too. It was Sarah.

'Come in,' he said.

They greeted one another with a warm familiarity.

Sarah clearly wanted to say something.

'Do you know, John,' she asked, 'that Adam is a smuggler?'

She looked out of the window and pointed at the Garden House. Cat had given her permission and John was the wisest person she knew.

32

The shallop had been adapted by Henry Calvert for work in rivers. He used rivers as his roads into Africa when he could. The shallop had lost its sails, and had had extra storage space built on. Eight slaves easily provided power for this shallow draughted boat.

In the hold some guns and gunpowder were placed first, but were soon hidden by barrels of brandy, rolls of cloth, swords, brass pans and crystal beads. Richard had carried in the pans, and Selina the three boxes of crystal beads.

She wished she could have some of the beautiful beads, but her mother had firmly taught her never to ask for what she wanted, and always to be grateful for what she had. 'You work or you weep' was one of her favourite comments.

The evening before as the last slaves were trading for the last time on African soil and were herded into the *Halifax's* canoes, Richard had run to his father, and asked him to buy back the little African boy.

'He was whipped because he tried to go with his mother. Then he was chained and whipped again. If he stayed here he could be a slave to Selina and me, and stay with his mother. He's still waiting by the riverside for the canoes to return.'

Henry was surprised. To him slaves were his business. They were like the cattle he had once worked with in England. You looked after them, fattened them to get the best price and sold them. Henry was proud of the way he looked after his slaves. They did not die of starvation or ill-treatment. He considered Richard's plea. He began to fear his son would never make a slave-trader.

'No,' he said.

Later Richard and Selina had crept down to the river themselves. They watched the guards laughing, drinking and gambling round the ten slaves chained to posts by the jetty.

72

'If we crept up, we might release him. He's at the end,' whispered Richard. He was determined to do something. They crept along the river bank. They were hardly hidden by the darkness which was pushed back by the light of the fire, but Richard relied on the power of their drink.

They were only three yards away, when the whiteness of their faces, legs and clothes gave them away.

The same sailor that had captured the slave boy rolled towards them with a gun and swearing. Then he saw who it was. He grabbed them both by the arm and took them back to the house. Drunk, he may have been, but he had guessed what the children were after, and he passed this on to their mother. She had risen from her bed when she heard the noise. She was not too ill to beat them and send them to bed.

But the next day that was forgotten as the slaves pushed off from the bank and they started to row up river towards King Ambo.

33

John Blackman was surprised. He put away his thoughts of love.

'Dear Sarah, you are too easily carried away by gossip. Sir Adam has as little need to smuggle as Sir Robert Walpole, and,' he added with a mischievous smile, 'between you and me I suspect he has not the mettle for it either.'

'I think, my dear John,' Sarah replied, 'he has not indeed enough metal. But it is metal of another kind.'

John laughed and considered the situation.

'The Kilmore Trading Company has two good ships and plantations in the West Indies. The profits have built this house.'

Sarah then explained the disasters which had fallen on the company. John's expression changed.

'Slave-trading had royal and church approval in the reign of Charles II. It still prospers and we must hope that the Kilmore Trading Company will again grow rich. But smuggling has much in common with slave-trading. Though in these German days Royal approval may not be forthcoming. I believe the church gives its blessing at times as long as the tithes are paid.'

'But smugglers are hanged.'

'Smugglers, dear Sarah, encourage free trade among countries, provide food and drink so that even the poor may live well, pay good tithes and provide work for labourers. And no-one suffers. It is not for us to ask Sir Adam where his money comes from. From us it would be a poor return for his generous hospitality. Let us indeed salute his courage.'

Sarah was not convinced. She sat silent.

'Come, Sarah. I have other things to say to you,' said the Rector.

34

Richard and Selina enjoyed the slow journey upstream. The river was sluggish and muddy. The sun shone through the jungle that overhung the river in a green light. Mosquitoes and flies followed the boat, but Richard and Selina did not notice them as they peered into the dark gaps in the jungle and listened to the howls of animals and the drumming from the villages hidden safely in the trees. They saw no-one. In this part of Sierra Leone it was dangerous for anyone to travel on his own or even with his family. Slave-traders had long, strong arms.

Henry, under a broad-brimmed hat made of palm leaves like his children, wearing a long white cotton coat, and dingy white slacks, was thinking how in his heart he disliked Africa. The heat oppressed him, and it was worse in the rainy season where a mustiness enclosed everything and mildew covered shoes, furniture, and any food left out. I am making eight hundred pounds a year he thought. If all goes well today I will go home and live as a gentleman of ease. He had seen much death in Sierra Leone and not only death of slaves, but death of the white traders. If disease did not kill then alcohol did. He knew the shanty the sailors sang had much truth in it.

'Beware and take care
Of the gulf of Benin
For the one that comes out
There are forty goes in.'

Henry thought, 'I shall be one that comes out.' He checked on his map as the river turned south. Two miles to go. He reached for his musket, and loaded it. It was the only gun to be seen on the boat. The princess had given him a clear picture of the manner in which King Ambo had to be approached.

'When I fire the gun you stand up and face the bank,' he ordered his slaves and children. Richard had already been

instructed. He was excited.

'Shall I salute the King?' He enjoyed watching sailors salute their officers.

'No,' said his father.

The jungle had retreated from the banks, and some corn was growing. Fishermen's nets were drying on the earth, and the thump of drums grew louder.

'Those drums are announcing our arrival,' commented Henry, half smiling.

'I can't see any palace,' said Selina, straining her eyes upstream. It was the first time she had been on a slaving expedition.

'I expect the King lives in that,' said Richard pointing to a small round hut built with upright tree trunks and a thatched roof. It had no door. Through the gap they could dimly see some children.

'Be quiet,' said his father. 'Do not speak when we land.'

Ahead a tall tree leant across the river. In front of it a large man, followed by two smaller men with spears was marching up and down.

'That's King Ambo,' said Henry quietly to the children. They could hardly believe their eyes.

King Ambo was indeed wearing a crown of brass, but under his large frightening face was a dirty naval officer's jacket on top of a white robe that was no cleaner.

Henry fired his musket over the great tree. The slaves left their oars and stood and so did the children.

King Ambo raised his silver head cane, and pointed to a spot on the bank. Henry ordered his slaves to row in.

35

Captain Matthew Kay was sitting in his small room in the dark and gloomy Sloop. His thoughts were equally dark and gloomy. With the help of his father he had purchased the post of Lieutenant of Dragoons, and with his own help had risen to be Captain. He had seen no battlefield. His disappointment at this was much the same as his Colonel's, who regarded the lack of a war as the most serious criticism you could make of a government. He said the Prime Minster, Sir Robert Walpole, was as fearful at the thought of war as his lady's maid was at the sight of a mouse.

He had not even marched north to fight the Jacobites. Then a month before Colonel Daniel Sear had finally told him his chance of honour had come. Honour makes every young soldier's heart leap, and Matthew's heart leapt.

It dived down again when he heard he would be sent to Sussex to aid the Justice of the Peace, the Officers of the Revenue and the Customs House men. Parliament had just passed a Smuggling Act increasing the penalty on those caught to hanging, and the army was ordered into action.

The Colonel suggested honour; his fellow officers in the mess suggested with greater reality that either they would shortly find him rich, or lying dead in the ditch.

The Colonel passed on to him information from a sworn statement by an arrested about-to-be-sentenced smuggler. The smuggler had received a free pardon and a reward, with which he had purchased an inn far from Sussex.

The River Ouse was Matthew's responsibility, and in particular he was required to investigate the Sloop Inn some fifteen miles from the coast. The information suggested that the innkeeper was at the heart of a profitable organization. The Captain was advised to contact the magistrate at Newick, Sir Charles Marsh, who had been surprisingly helpful. He did not think Samuel Jebb would be involved.

'He's from an old Sussex family,' he said. From what Matthew had heard this was not particularly encouraging information, but nevertheless Sir Charles had suggested he took his men and investigated the Sloop. More than that. He promised to accompany him and to investigate the inn himself, if Matthew could delay for two days so that he could fulfil his magistrate's duties.

Matthew was glad to have a magistrate with him. He felt that he was in a different country in Sussex, and the natives were not friendly.

The first visit had interested Matthew. Samuel Jebb, though clearly a hard, surly man, had made some effort to welcome him. His men had been given a pint of Sussex ale before they investigated the building. Matthew refused the drink. He needed to be alert. He went through the cellars and barns behind.

'I think we have seen nothing suspicious here,' said Sir Charles as they climbed up from a second large empty cellar. 'Sam's too busy with his ale, to take the risk of smuggling. Magistrates are some of his best drinkers,' Sir Charles ended with a laugh.

'Does he farm at all?'

'Farm? Samuel?' again Sir Charles laughed. 'Samuel has never tilled a foot of land nor milked a cow in all his days.'

Matthew made a second investigation with his men the next day. He wrote down his thoughts afterwards.

1. Why were all the cellars and barns so empty?
2. Why was there sheep's wool in the dust on the floor of the cellars? Matthew had learnt all about owlers exporting wool, while importing tea, coffee, spirits and tobacco. His Colonel had been efficient.
3. And was this tea? He had picked up a handful of dust from the other cellar as he was about to follow Sir Charles. He had put it in his handkerchief. When he unwrapped it there were three small black fragments of leaf in the dust. He thought it was tea.
4. His men had found six empty large rowing boats and the twenty yards of path from the river to the barn had a better surface than the road along which

he had come from Scaynes Hill.
5. Sir Charles had said that Samuel wouldn't take a risk. Matthew disagreed.

Matthew began to scent honour ahead.

He rode over to Newick, and presented his evidence to Sir Charles Marsh. Matthew felt Sir Charles seemed more surprised than pleased.

'Captain Kay,' he said finally. 'You may have discovered important evidence; on the other hand you may be wrong. It would be unwise to write to your Colonel now, as you wish. A wrong report might ruin your career. You have done your duty and have informed me. My advice is now to stay at the Sloop and get to know Samuel Jebb and his ways better.

Matthew agreed but reluctantly. Catching honour was difficult.

36

Henry Calvert, Richard, Selina and then Sam and the other slaves jumped out of the boat. Sam tied it between some twenty war canoes which also played an important part in slave-trading.

Henry led Richard and Selina to King Ambo. Henry and Richard bowed slightly. Selina curtsied. The King smiled and raised his cane towards them in a gesture of apparent approval. A memory came back to Henry of his young days in church when a bishop had held his hand over him in a blessing. He was careful not to smile as they followed King Ambo back to what Selina supposed would be his palace.

A hundred yards from the bank was the largest house of the village. There was a low covered platform in front and behind three openings, through which the children could see movements, and the flash of eyes in the dim light.

On the platform was a large wooden chair. King Ambo went to sit on it. It was his throne. He waved his stick. Three women scuttled from the dark interior and laid on the floor six feet in front of the throne three threadbare pieces of carpet. The King pointed to them and the Calvert family sat down uncomfortably.

Henry realized that he was not in the best position for bargaining, but he realized too that he had no choice. Richard and Selina were fascinated by the palace. On the wall behind the King were stuck human skulls, the skins of birds, pieces of flags and feathers. The women who had brought the carpets knelt before the King with terror in their eyes. A wave of the stick sent them scurrying back into the dark holes.

All had been silent except for a quiet background throb of drums.

The two bargainers eyed each other. They both thought the other was crafty, villainous and fraudulent.

King Ambo spoke in clear English.

'I want three things, guns and ball and brandy. I have three things for you, men, women and children.' He raised his stick. His two attendants who crouched behind the throne, rose and disappeared round the large hut. The drums beat louder.

King Ambo rose.

'We eat. We eat first. My wives bring food. Then slaves and guns.'

Richard and Selina were excited. A meal with a king, even though the King himself disappointed their expectations, was wonderful. The food when the worried wives came scurrying out again was not so wonderful. First a big bowl of boiled, stringy hens reeking of wood smoke was offered to Ambo. He took what looked like a whole bird, and put it on a large china plate, handed to him by another wife. A third wife came with a large bowl of rice. The fourth wife came with another bowl of a dark green mushy vegetable which was going to be the children's first introduction to spinach.

The Calverts were then offered the same food. They did not eat as heartily as the King, but Richard and Selina appreciated being given the choice of what they ate and how much there was of it. They were given no such choice at home.

There was no conversation during the meal until Ambo had finished his eating and had tossed to the floor the bones of the fowl, which were instantly removed by dark arms from within the hut. Then a younger wife appeared clutching a big stone jug, which she poured into a silver tankard which Ambo held out.

'Best Madeira wine. Very best,' he said. Henry was given a tankard and the younger and clearly favoured wife poured wine for him too. Ambo's big face was smiling, and Henry judged the time ripe for business.

He said thank you for the meal, and asked about the slaves and their prices.

'You see slaves. You look.'

He banged his stick twice on the floor. The clink of chains could be heard and in less than a minute, Henry saw the slaves.

The first column of men were tied in pairs round their necks with lianas. Their hands were secured behind their backs. They walked slowly with their heads down. Ambo's assistant had changed his spear for a whip and guided them round in front of the hut.

'Good strong slaves,' said Ambo. Henry had to agree. He saw why Ambo had his reputation with slave-traders. Some sixty passed and then disappeared behind the hut. Richard could hear them being chained again.

Then came the women. They too were tied round the neck but their hands were free. Little children, some Richard and Selina's age followed. Some children were on their mother's backs. Despair took all life from the faces of the women though there was still hope in the children's eyes. All the slaves were naked.

The whole scene made an impression on Richard and Selina that neither of them would forget for the rest of their lives.

Henry realized he would indeed be rich if he could make a good deal. He also realized that it was not going to be easy unless he offered guns. He could see that the princess had indeed spoken sense over not giving Ambo guns. The King was clearly ruthless, with considerable organizing skill. His ambitions were growing and he would deal with the whites for only as long as he had to. With guns he would become a slave-trader himself.

The bargaining began. Henry sent his slaves to bring his goods. They returned with a barrel of brandy, a gleaming sword, some metal jugs and pans and bales of cloth. They were placed in front of Ambo. He looked with interest. He picked up the sword, and swept it through the air.

Henry thought all was going well.

Ambo smiled; then his expression changed.

'Guns,' he said. 'Where are the guns?'

'No guns,' Henry replied, 'but I have other goods. '

He turned and walked away to his slaves. As he walked Richard saw Ambo motion towards his other attendant with a spear.

His slave sprang up, ran past Richard and Selina, raised his spear and plunged it into Henry's back. Henry gasped, fell forward, and lay motionless on the ground, dead.

37

Sarah was at home again in Whitechapel

Life which had been passing simply and sweetly was now full of problems, as if from being a shallow sparkling stream flowing through the fields and flowers, it had suddenly become a rushing torrent bouncing over rocks and down waterfalls.

Peggy had written a letter saying she was ill, and Sarah knew well that Peggy must be really ill if she admitted it.

Katharine was distraught with worry over money and the knowledge that Sir Adam was a smuggler.

The Rector of Barcombe had proposed to Sarah, and she had asked for time to think about it.

John Wesley had had tea with her and had made it clear that her income, her house and her other delights in life came from something evil – slavery.

'Oh, John,' she cried. 'You always bring me bad news. Cannot you bring me good news?'

'Good news, dear Sarah is the one thing I have to bring.'

'Good news? Oh you're going to preach a sermon.'

'No, not a sermon. I just wanted to pass on a gift. A gift of salvation to all who have faith – a gift that will take you from hell, help you to deal with your problems and give . . . .'

'It is a sermon. I already have faith. I believe all the things I should.'

'Faith is not an opinion, nor any number of opinions put together even if they were all true. A string of opinions is no more Christian faith than a string of beads is Christian holiness.'

'I believe in the creed I say in church. You cannot find anything wrong with that,' said Sarah aggressively.

John Wesley could.

'A man may assent to three or three and twenty creeds and yet have no Christian faith at all.'

'The Rector of Barcombe is right. You say all the Church of England is wrong and you alone know the truth.'

Sarah was getting cross. She spent her time with John Blackman justifying John Wesley, and her time with John Wesley justifying John Blackman.

'No, Sarah. I love the Church of England, and in one of its homilies you have the true definition of faith. "A sure trust and confidence which a man has in God, that through the merits of Christ, his sins are forgiven, and he reconciled to the favour of God." That is the good news.'

'I can't match you with talking, John, but I think you will not persuade me.'

'Perhaps not, Sarah, but I pray the Holy Spirit will.'

38

Richard and Selina stood motionless. Then Selina rushed forward and knelt by Henry's side crying, 'Get up, father. Get up.'

But she knew as everybody else did that her father was dead.

'You have murdered him,' shouted Richard running to the man, whose spear was still in his father's back, and hitting him with his fists.

Selina looked round in tears.

'Don't, Richard, don't,' she pleaded. 'They will kill you too.'

Sam stepped forward and pulled the spear from Henry's back, leaving a growing red stain on his white shirt.

The killer held Richard away from him, but did not hurt him.

King Ambo suddenly spoke in a language the children did not understand. There was instant activity. Some more men rushed forward, lifted Henry's body and began carrying it to the river bank.

Richard tried to escape from the soldier holding him.

'No, no. Leave him. We shall take him home.' He wrenched himself clear and rushed to the other soldiers. One of them knocked him down. Selina rose and ran to help him. She beat her fists against the soldier and cried in fury.

King Ambo stepped towards Richard who was getting up.

'Don't touch him,' screamed Selina. 'Run, Richard.'

Ambo's big hand gripped Richard's shoulder.

Selina rushed and attacked the King pummelling his large belly with her hands. Ambo dropped his stick and seized Selina with the other hand.

He lifted them both in the air effortlessly. He looked at them both, as they struggled silent now. Then King Ambo smiled, and put them both down. They stood before him angry and afraid and sore and helpless. For five seconds there was silence.

Richard looked round to see where Sam and his father's slaves were, and wondered whether they could fight. He saw they were all held by Ambo's soldiers and that each one had another soldier behind him with a raised spear.

Richard looked up at the smiling Ambo, and decided that he and Selina were about to be killed as their father had. Selina was thoughtless with rage and was just about to start hitting Ambo again, when he spoke.

'Brave. I like you. You brave boy and girl.'

The children were silent, stunned at these words from the most evil man they knew in the world.

'We bury your father. Good grave. He brave man. We bury him.'

He picked up his stick, and spoke briskly in his own tongue. There was once again an immediate response. Henry's slaves who did not understand the language were led down to the shallop still with spears at their backs. The four soldiers carrying Henry's body started to move again along the path by the river.

King Ambo looked at the children.

'You eat,' he said and indeed two of his wives were coming out with a bowl of grapes and pomegranates.

'No,' said Richard half in tears. 'We will see our father buried. We will go with them.'

King Ambo smiled again.

'Go with them,' he said. 'Brave boy and girl.'

Richard and Selina followed the soldiers along the wet path by the river. The dark jungle closed around them. In half a mile the path opened out on to a patch of scrub land, where there had been some cultivation. There twenty yards from the river was a hole dug, and with a pile of soil on the far side. The soldiers carried the body there and put it in. It was only later that Richard and Selina realized what this already dug grave meant. At present all they could do was to stand in tears as a soldier pushed soil over their father with a spade. Then unseen a new man stood by the grave. He was masked, and dressed in a long cloak made of a mixture of feathers and raffia. He began to mutter and pour oil on the half-covered body.

Richard's grief was suddenly overcome by anger. He realized it was a witch-doctor.

'No,' he shouted and rushed forward to the witch-doctor. He

grabbed the jug and threw it away. The witch-doctor stood back and did nothing. Nor did Ambo's soldiers.

'Come on, Selina,' said Richard. 'We'll have a proper Christian service.'

'But we don't know what to do,' sobbed Selina.

'We'll say the Lord's Prayer that our mother taught us. You remember that?'

'Yes.'

Richard grabbed Selina's hand and they said the Lord's Prayer together beside their father's grave.

The witch-doctor disappeared into the jungle as quietly as he had come. The soldiers dug more earth into the grave.

'We'll make a cross,' said Selina. Richard found two sticks which they bound together with strong grass. The grave had been covered. Richard stuck the cross in firmly. They looked at it sadly.

'Come on,' said Richard. 'We must tell mother.'

They set off down the path to Ambo's village. The soldiers followed.

Sam and his father's slaves were still being held by soldiers. On the shallop Ambo's men were searching and carrying off all they found. They placed them in front of Ambo who again sat on his throne.

A great smile lit Ambo's face as he looked at his booty. Selina saw the beads she had longed for. Richard saw the last searchers leave the boat with the guns and the powder. Ambo stood up with delight as he saw what they were.

'Guns,' he said. 'Guns. Your father said no guns. He had guns. Now King Ambo has guns.'

'They are ours,' said Richard.

King Ambo did not seem to understand.

'I like you,' he said to the children. 'You safe. You go home.' He rapped out some commands. At once Sam and the slaves were released. Richard and Selina followed them into the boat.

'Goodbye,' shouted King Ambo.

The children did not reply as the slaves pushed off from the bank and began to row downstream.

'I hate him, I hate him,' said Selina, crying again.

Richard was thinking. His father had sailed into a trap. The grave was ready for him. Then another thought came to him.

How kind Ambo and the Africans had been to them. It would have cost him nothing to kill them and he would have gained eight slaves and a boat.

'I hate him too,' he replied. 'But we are still alive.'

39

On the day that Henry Calvert was murdered both Captain Kay and Parson Chipperfield learnt something interesting about smugglers.

It was harvest time. Even the farmers admitted it had been a good year especially for barley. The summer had been hot and dry, and the price of sheep had increased since the North had suffered from an icy February.

Parson Chipperfield was asked to be present at the Harvest Supper at Roots Barn to give the blessing. He sat with Farmer Cornwell who owned much of the land around Barcombe. With him were his wife and four children enjoying the magnificent meal that they had provided.

The conversation was lively. The farmer argued about prices. Wheat was as high as it had ever been. Then some Sussex songs were sung and Sussex ale was drunk. Then the Parson noted some of the farm hands in heated discussion, and several of them kept nodding in his direction. At last one bolder than the rest shouted across the table, 'Parson Chipperfield, you are a learned man. Would you grant us reply to a religious dispute we are having?'

The Parson was delighted. He had always longed to instruct his congregation in the delights of theology, but they seemed reluctant to listen.

'I shall be happy to give my opinion, Simon Gaydon, on the point in dispute.'

Why, sir,' replied Simon, 'we wish to know if there were not sins which God Almighty would not forgive.'

The Parson was taken aback, but replied that he trusted there were no sins, that they were liable to do, which if the sinner repented and resolved not to do again, would not be forgiven by God. He was disappointed that this reply did not altogether satisfy the group, so he added, 'What kind of sin was so dreadful that there was no hope of God's pardon?'

There was no hesitation in the farm hand's reply.

'Why, sir, we thought that if a man should find out where goods from the sea were held, and should inform a Customs Inspector, then indeed such a villain was too bad for mercy.'

Everyone was listening now. Parson Chipperfield knew well enough what goods from the sea were.

There was a five second silence, and then the jovial farmer Cornwell called for another song and the beautiful Susan Frost sang a haunting love song about the Ouse.

The sad ending brought tears to the eyes of the guests, but not to Parson Chipperfield's. He was thinking hard.

Captain Kay had not been invited to the Harvest Supper. He was sitting drinking happily with Samuel Jebb. He could not have foreseen this happy evening. The magistrate, Sir Charles Marsh, had used his influence to get a room for him and a barn for his men at the Sloop. As Sir Charles had said, 'That will give you an opportunity to find out what Jebb is up to. It will be to your advantage when your Colonel receives your report on the Sloop.'

At first the Captain had not enjoyed the company of the surly innkeeper. However over the weeks his surliness had lessened, and the Captain realized that in the unlikely event of the innkeeper being innocent he at least would know the secrets of the smugglers and such was Jebb's love of money, he would doubtless be prepared to reveal them at a price.

That evening while the bar was full all the dragoons had been filled with ale and now slept happily in the barn. The Captain too was in an optimistic if slightly hazy state of mind, and was pondering whether to go downstairs and challenge the innkeeper to reveal the truth about smuggling. In fact he raised himself with difficulty and crossed to the door. Here he hit his head sharply on the low crossbeam and returned to his chair rubbing the injured part. Tomorrow, he thought, I will find out the truth.

But then there was a knock on the door, and in stooped the innkeeper with a jug.

'Ah, Captain,' he said. 'A drink to sleep on.' He poured two tankards of brandy, and sat on the Captain's narrow bed.

Fate had led him into my hand, thought the Captain cheerfully as he sipped the excellent brandy.

91

'Jebb,' he said. 'I want the truth.'

The innkeeper seemed surprised. He pulled a paper from his pocket. It looked like an account.

'Here's the truth, Captain,' he replied. 'You and your men drank well tonight, but because of my friendship to you I have charged you but one tenth of the price. See here, and he pointed to the total one shilling.'

Captain Kay had hoped it was free, but certainly one shilling was a generous price, and as he felt he was about to solve the Sussex smuggling problem, he gave his thanks.

'Could you sign?' asked the innkeeper, rising and collecting ink from the Captain's desk.

'With much appreciation,' murmured the Captain, and he gave a confident signature at the foot of the page, not noticing there was much on the sheet apart from the account.

The innkeeper snatched it away.

'What is the truth,' asked the Captain slowly in a rather slurred voice, 'about smuggling at the Sloop?'

'It is time for you to sleep, Captain. The truth is that you have been drinking smuggled goods, and you have signed that you knew you were drinking smuggled goods. We shall talk in the morning, but sleep now, because it may be a noisy night.'

With an effort the Captain rose. He knew something was not right. He stepped towards the door, staggered and fell on his bed, the remains of his brandy spilling across the room.

On the table lay the innkeeper's untouched tankard. The innkeeper closed the door behind him and then locked it.

Down below in the inn another group of men were gathering, and horses and wagons were waiting outside.

40

The journey home to the mouth of the river was long and quiet and slow for Richard and Selina. Richard clasped Selina who lay half asleep. They sat where their father had sat on the journey upstream. The air was sultry and full of mosquitoes. The long creeping mangrove roots seemed to Richard to be trying to catch their boat and in the dark green light on the jungle frightening crashes could be heard, and the throb of village drums beat to the background rhythm of the cicadas.

The river Camaranca broadened and Richard saw his home silhouetted against the flaming red and orange of the sun as it fell below the horizon.

Sam tied the boat to the jetty. The children ran to the house. Their mother was still in bed and was as white as the sheet she lay on.

Richard blurted out the news. His mother covered her face with her hands. There was a silence. She put her hands on the bed and Selina took one and grasped it. She noticed her mother did not cry. At last Peggy Calvert spoke.

'You must go to England. I will write. My sisters will look after you.'

'You must come to England too,' said Richard.

'No,' said Peggy. 'My duty is here. I shall do what your father would have done.'

Then she started to ask questions. The whole story was laid before including the ready grave and the witch-doctor.

'I should have realized,' said Peggy slowly. 'Your father was purposely killed by an evil man. You must go to England quickly.'

'How shall we go? You are too ill, mother. Shall I get Sam to take me to Mr Clow? He could arrange it.'

A flush came into Peggy's cheeks. 'No, no,' she cried. 'We shall find someone. Go and eat and find Sam for me.'

41

Eugene Chipperfield had from his youth intended to be a good man. His father had fought in the army under the Duke of Marlborough, and he loved re-telling the stories of Blenheim, Oudenarde and Malplaquet as he drank and gambled his fortune away on the cards and horses. He had named his son after the prince who fought with Marlborough but to Captain Chipperfield's dismay his son, Eugene, showed no signs of copying his brave namesake. Eugene hated fighting. He did not like horses.

One day when the Captain was teaching the young men of the village to use a sword, he discovered that Eugene had disappeared. With his sword and his pupils' swords (two pieces of wood tied together), the warriors searched the village to find him, and having found him reading a book behind the haystack, they all chased him round the village prodding him none too gently with their swords.

The delight of the chase took away the Captain's fury, and when after a happy evening at the inn, he found his exhausted son Eugene at home, he said, 'You are a milksop. You are fit for nothing but the church.'

Eugene had not thought of this before, but he soon warmed to the idea.

There was no fighting, if you joined the church. There were not many books in the Captain's house, but one was the Bible and Eugene had been spellbound by the character of Jesus. There was no-one else like him. He studied hard.

And so, here he was, a curate at Barcombe, living in a large, cold house with a wife and three children. He found the people of Barcombe poor and suspicious. They spread stories of him not going to church when it rained, and Eugene knew to his cost that this rumour had reached the Rector. The cause of the story was that a fever had struck him suddenly on Saturday, and though his wife and children had gone to St Mary's with a message, the rumour still spread.

Eugene visited the poor and as the years went by, he did gain some respect. However in his heart he was not satisfied with himself. He decided he spent far too much time worrying about money, which Jesus never did, and that he was a coward, which Jesus wasn't.

Then at the Harvest Supper he discovered that some of his congregation were smugglers. He decided that he must be brave. He must put a stop to it.

He felt that the best thing he could do would be to ask the Rector for advice.

Nine miles up river at the Sloop, Captain Matthew Kay was in despair. His memories of the evening before were vague, but innkeeper Jebb had come up bearing some ale for breakfast. As Matthew drank, Jebb reminded him of what he had signed the night before.

'There's as many on the gallows for using smuggled goods as there are for smuggling it,' said the innkeeper with his hard, wrinkled face creasing into a grin.

This was not true, but the captain had not enough assurance in his muddled mind to challenge it.

'What are you going to do about it?' asked Jebb brutally. 'Riches or gallows?'

Back came to him the words of his fellow officers, 'rich or lying dead in a ditch'. How right they were.

'I want your answer,' said the innkeeper who had watched the pale captain for a minute of silence.

'I do not know,' replied Captain Kay.

'That is not a wise answer. I shall be back in two hours for a better answer.'

The captain heard the lock turned in the door outside. He clasped his head in his hands and realized that 'dead in a ditch' was still a possibility.

42

An ill Peggy Calvert was more than able to keep their small slave factory going. She dragged herself from bed and made short boat journeys to the points where bedraggled slaves from up the coast were led in. She took the children with her and Sam became a servant instead of a slave.

Richard and Selina began to see their world in a new light. They saw filthy, swearing white men carried at the front of slave coffles while other whites or black servants whipped the line of roped and usually naked slaves. Selina tried to interfere when she saw a half-drunk white trader branding a little girl about her age. Her mother sternly called her back.

None of the slaves Peggy Calvert bought was branded but mothers and children were tied and the men chained together. They were taken back by boat to the Camaranca river to await purchase by the next ship's captain.

One day when the Calverts were about to depart with six new slaves, there was much shouting and swearing beside them.

'Too much rum, and too little sense,' said Peggy Calvert, who felt she had done better slave-bargaining than any of these loud-mouthed men.

Richard and Selina looked round.

'It's John Newton,' cried Selina, and the children ran to the group. There was John Newton upright, in cleaner clothes and half drunk. He was quarrelling with the white trader he had bought his slaves from. He swore at him, and raised his fist.

Selina grabbed the other hand and clung on.

John stopped shouting.

'Think of Polly,' shouted Selina.

John Newton looked down. His face changed.

'It's Selina,' he cried, and lifted her up above his head.

'Here is the girl who saved me from the princess of hell,' he shouted.

Peggy rushed over and ordered John to put her down at once.

Introductions followed from Richard. Then explanations. Then they found common ground in their opinion of Mrs Clow.

Before long John Newton promised he would find a way for the children to travel to England. Peggy found he had some connection with the navy. She did not wish her children to go to Liverpool or Bristol via the West Indies or the slave ships.

John Newton kissed Selina as they departed for Camaranca in their boat. Selina loved him but she was perfectly happy to be second choice to Polly.

43

John Blackman was again in Barcombe in the late Autumn. So was Sarah.

John wished to see Sarah, to advise Sir Adam and to avoid his curate, who would be in Kilmore House tutoring George.

'He will be after my money,' said John, 'and I fear he will never make a gentleman. A gentleman should of course have money, but he should never ask for it.'

'I have a story for you about another parson,' interrupted Sarah. 'I want to know your opinion.'

'Did you learn of it from Wesley?' asked John suspiciously. 'If you did, I want none of your story.'

'No,' replied Sarah in beautiful innocence. 'Not a word from Wesley. I believe, in fact, that the story-teller did not like Wesley overmuch.'

'Then he is a friend of mine,' said John. 'I shall hear the story.'

'There was once a clergyman called Cognatus,' said Sarah in her sweetest voice, 'who was sober, had a good reputation in his parish and in the world. All his parishioners thought him an honest man and very expert at making a bargain. The farmers listened to him with attention when he spoke of the best time of selling corn. He had for twenty years watched the markets and had raised for himself a considerable fortune.

'Now our Cognatus is very orthodox with a great esteem for our Prayer Book services; and if he has not prayers on Wednesday and Friday it is because his predecessor had not used the parish to any such custom.

'As he cannot serve all his livings he makes it a matter to keep sober curates in them, at as cheap a rate as sober men can be procured.

'Cognatus has always been prosperous yet he still had the uneasiness and vexations of those who are deep in worldly business. Taxes, losses, bad mortgages, bad tenants and the hardness of the times are frequent subjects of his conversation, and have a great effect on his spirits.

'He has no other end in growing rich, but that he may leave a considerable fortune to his niece whom he has politely educated in expensive finery by what he has saved out of the tithes of his livings.'

'Ah, there your story or rather sermon falls down,' said John pleasantly. 'I have no niece.'

'Do not interrupt my sermon, if such it be. I shall go on reading,' replied Sarah equally pleasantly. 'Now the neighbours looked on Cognatus as a happy clergyman because they see him in good circumstances. Some neighbours want to dedicate their sons to the church, because Cognatus has risen, when his father was but an ordinary man.'

'I am beginning to like this Cognatus,' said John. 'He is a worthy man.'

'I think perhaps he is a worthy man. It is possible that he is a man I love a little,' said Sarah sweetly.

John looked at her, and blushed perhaps for the first time in his life.

'But do not interrupt me again. That is indeed not worthy of a gentleman. My sermon reaches its climax soon. Now, if Cognatus, when he first entered into holy orders, had perceived how absurd a thing it is to grow rich by the Gospel; if he had followed St Augustine who dared not enrich any of his relations out of the revenue of the church; if instead of twenty years care to lay up treasures upon earth, he had given his money in charity and compassion; if instead of tempting his niece to be proud, he had clothed, comforted and assisted widows, orphans and the distressed, who were all to appear for him on the last day; if instead of the anxieties of troublesome mortgages and ill bargains, he had the comfort of knowing that his treasure was securely laid up, where neither the moth corrupts, nor thieves break through and steal.'

'I think, Sarah, we have had enough. Perhaps I detect the subtlety of a Wesley,' suggested John.

'No, you shall hear me and my story-teller, William Law, to the end. Sit down again in your comfortable pew and listen.

'If our Cognatus instead of having many livings had thought it wrong for a clergyman to traffic for gain in holy things; if he had recommended honest labour to his niece rather than support her in idleness by the labours of curates; if this had been the spirit would he have lost any happiness? Could it be said that life thus governed by the spirit of the Gospel must be dull and melancholy, if compared to that of raising a fortune for a niece?'

John now recognized the piece which he had read in his young days. 'I am happy I have no niece, and I fear without a niece your sermon falls rather flat.'

'Mr Blackman, Mr Blackman,' came a loud voice from outside. 'May I have the honour of a word with you?'

Irritation wrinkled John's face.

'It's Eugene after more money again. I must escape Sarah, by this other door.'

Sarah laughed.

'You may not have a niece, John, but you have a curate or two.'

There was a knock on the door.

John made a quick exit by the other door.

44

Richard and Selina only had one more month at their Camaranca home for John Newton, the slave-trader remembered his promise to Peggy Calvert and appeared in his boat with news that HMS *Harwich* was lying off the coast and would take the children to Plymouth.

The Sierra Leone was the only life that Richard and Selina knew. There were tears when they said goodbye to their mother, Sam and the other house-slaves, but there was excitement too. England had been portrayed to them by all who were making a grim living in the hot, steamy and unhealthy Guinea coast as the promised land.

They took with them letters addressed to Lady Kilmore, and Miss Sarah Crossman.

John Newton did not take them out to the ship, but provided a boat and two trusted slaves.

Captain Cripps received them kindly. When Richard mentioned John Newton, the Captain's kindly expression changed.

'I have taken you,' he said solemnly, 'because I know John Newton's father. He is a good man.'

As the dark green line of Sierra Leone faded from their eyes, Richard and Selina clasped hands, partly in joy and partly in grief.

They enjoyed the journey to Plymouth, and neither of them was sea-sick.

To the end of her days Selina said the two sets of people who were kindest to children were black Africans and sailors.

45

'Come in,' called Sarah.

Eugene Chipperfield came in, and was taken aback just to see Sarah. He was full of apologies, but she cut him short, and offered him a seat.

Surprised Eugene sat down.

'Is your message for the Rector important?' asked Sarah.

'I fear it is,' said Eugene. 'It is about . . . ' but then he felt he couldn't go on and was covered in confused embarrassment.

'Is it about money?' asked Sarah sweetly.

'Money,' Eugene was taken by surprise. 'No, not really money. Well, I suppose money comes into it, but . . . .'

Sarah was now intrigued.

'Into your stipend which I believe the Rector pays?'

Eugene was more confused.

'No, no, not my stipend. It's not that.'

Sarah changed tactics. She held up a book which she pulled out of an embroidered bag by the chair. It was, *A Serious Call to a Devout and Holy Life* by William Law. She rose and gave it to him.

Eugene rose, accepted it with thanks and sat down feeling completely out of his depth with this beautiful, unusual lady.

'Have you read it?'

Eugene pulled himself together. At last he could give a sensible answer.

'Yes, I have read it. I found it a most helpful and inspiring book.'

'So did I,' replied Sarah pleased. 'I found it more lively and amusing, than I feared I would from the title.'

Eugene remembered that as a young man the seriousness of the book had influenced him towards being a clergyman, and was about to say this when Sarah spoke again.

'You teach, my nephew, George, do you not?'

'Yes, Miss Crossman.'

'Do you enjoy teaching?'

'It gives me great pleasure to instruct George,' replied Eugene truthfully.

'I have a letter in Whitechapel from my sister in Africa, whose husband has just died and who intends to send her two children, a boy of eleven and a girl of ten home, for education. Would you be willing to teach them with George?'

Eugene considered the matter.

'Well, if Sir Adam were happy with such an arrangement.'

'Sir Adam will certainly be happy,' remarked Sarah sharply.

'Yes, I would be happy to teach them.'

'I would like to make a payment to you of twenty pounds a year for your extra duties,' said Sarah.

Eugene could hardly believe his ears. Gratitude flooded him, but she cut him short.

'I shall let you know when the children arrive. It may be a month or two. I shall inform the Rector you wish to speak to him. Goodbye, Mr Chipperfield.'

A happy curate departed, but he had not forgotten his purpose in seeing the Rector. He would return the next day.

Lady Katharine had also received a letter, for Peggy knew only half the letters sent from Africa arrived at the destination to which they were addressed in England. Her letter to Lady Katharine was sent via Captain Cripps on HMS *Harwich* and reached its destination a week after the ship reached Plymouth.

Katharine hurried to her husband and told him that Richard and Selina were awaiting transport to Sussex from Plymouth.

Sir Adam was in despair again. His crest was forgotten. He had already used the four hundred and fifty pounds sent from the Camaranca which he had promised the Calverts to use for school fees. The money that he needed to live as a gentleman took every penny he could get. He still hoped to send George away to school, but there could be no places for Richard and Selina. He must stop them coming.

'For a short time, Lady Katharine, it will be better if those children stay where they are.'

'But, Sir Adam, they know no-one there. Peggy expects us to look after them and provide for their education.'

'I fear the expectations of your sister may not be carried out

103

immediately. Winter is coming and it is too dangerous for two little children to travel by coach.' Sir Adam was warming to his theme; he could not afford to be a protector of these African brats.

'I can easily find a good home for them over the winter. I shall find a suitable school for them later.'

Lady Katharine, though not entirely satisfied with this, accepted her husband's proposal. She had secretly felt that these two children brought up without the benefits of civilization would be ignorant and uncouth and would not be a helpful influence to George.

She considered the situation. She decided she would not tell Sarah at present. Sarah had always been inclined to interfere.

46

It was on the Rector's last day in the parish of Barcombe before his return to London that his Curate finally cornered him. The Rector was cantering back from a visit to an old friend in Lewes, when the Curate had seen him entering the gates. The Curate praised George for his work, gathered up his books, and hurried out of the porch to find Fred holding the horse and John Blackman dismounting.

'Ah, Eugene,' the Rector cried out, trying to slip past him into the house. The Curate stepping smartly to one side blocked the half open door, and firmly told his tale of the Harvest Supper. John's pleasure at finding there were no further demands on his money, was then lessened by further requests for advice about smuggling. He was surprised too. He considered that Eugene though good value for cost as a curate, was indeed a feeble and fragile man with little intellect and less courage.

'Come inside,' he said. He led Eugene into the small room which was used as George's schoolroom, and they both sat down at the table.

John looked at his curate with a smile as he considered his tactics.

'Smuggling,' he said. 'Smuggling! Now what is smuggling? In this age of reason we must take care, Eugene, that our emotions do not overwhelm us. You must understand that what you call "smuggling", might by someone else be called "free-trade". And free-trade surely is a worthy occupation.'

He looked at Eugene but could not read his thoughts. He continued, 'And there are two further considerations that are telling points. Why should our unworthy King interfere with the good drink of his subjects? Should an Englishman give up his rights or should he fight for them?

'And, Eugene, one of your duties is to care for all of your

parishioners – the rich and the poor, is it not?'

'Yes, Rector.'

'It is possible there is some truth in what you heard at the Harvest Supper – though it is also possible it was just drunken farmhand's boasts – but if there is some truth in it, think about this. The farmers around here are poor; they cannot pay more than ten shillings a week to their labourers. Now is that enough for a labourer with a wife and, say, four children?'

Eugene agreed with some enthusiasm that it certainly was not.

'That being so, it would indeed be harsh if you were to take from these poor wives and little children the extra money that these labourers earn from smuggling, from free-trade. Indeed it could not be said that the divine Son of God would approve of such mean-spirited behaviour.'

John leant back in his chair with some satisfaction. Eugene was silent.

'Thus, Eugene, experience and reason will combine to show you that it is not your business to involve yourself in such matters. I shall bid you good evening. We shall meet again in December when I shall return to Kilmore House.'

Eugene rose, and left the room. As he walked down the drive, he muttered to himself, 'But smuggling is wrong, smuggling is wrong.'

47

Captain Cripps liked Richard and Selina.

He took them with him to the King's Head in Plymouth. The ten days the *Harwich* was to spend in Devonport harbour gave him no opportunity of reaching his home in Penrith. He wrote to his wife and told her of the children he was looking after. He had always been sad that they had had no children.

Richard and Selina loved their introduction to England. Devon sunshine, a kindly Captain who taught them to ride, and new exciting food made Camaranca seem another world.

After a week a midshipman brought Captain Cripps a letter he was expecting. He had shown the children the Exeter coach which left daily from the King's Head, and had told them that soon they would be travelling on it.

'Captain G. Cripps

HMS *Harwich*

Sir,

Lady Katharine wishes to join me in rendering our heartfelt thanks to you for your inestimable kindness in bringing back safely from Africa our dear nephew and niece.

I would I could come to Plymouth to accompany them to Sussex, but I fear my duties here press heavily on me, and Lady Katharine will not consent to the children being sent alone on a coach. We have heard too many dreadful stories, as indeed you will have too, about the type of people who use coaches and the dangers that arise on such journeys.

With winter now approaching the roads will be impassable. In spite of difficulties and dangers I would even have come myself had it not been for the advice of my great friend, Sir Charles Marsh, the magistrate at Newick.

Because of his philanthropy he knows of an excellent "Home for Foundlings" at Crown Hill not far from Plymouth. You will know the sad truth that the children's father is dead and their mother is ill. They will therefore be gladly accepted, looked after and taught there, and there could be no better place for them to live until we come and take them to Kilmore House.

I should be grateful if you would take them to the "Home for Foundlings". I have written to Mr Shillibeer, who is the master there, to expect their arrival.

Yours etc.

Adam Kilmore.'

It is absurd, thought the Captain, that I am worried about two little children. But he was. He did not understand the letter. There were many ways which the Captain could see, in which the children could be safely taken to Sussex. A coachman, at a price, would guard the children as closely as her Ladyship would wish.

The Captain wished he had more time ashore but he had to be back on his ship in two days. He would have to do what Sir Adam had asked.

He told the children as cheerfully as he could, and was impressed with them for the happy acceptance with which they took it.

'We have one more day together,' he said. 'We'll ride down to the sea and I'll teach you how to climb rocks.'

☆   ☆   ☆

Edmund Shillibeer was pleased with the letter from Sir Adam Kilmore. His service under Sir Charles in the army had done him much good. Though Edmund had never been a success as a soldier he had had sharp eyes and a quick ear for gossip. When he left the army he sought a post as a gardener for Sir Charles. When this was not granted, he pointed out that there were various things he knew that perhaps Lady Marsh was unaware of.

Thus in a very short time he found himself in a comfortable position as far from Newick as Sir Charles could manage. Sir Ernest Blain had left money in his will for a Master of a 'House for Foundlings in the West Country'. Sir Charles was chief of the trustees and Edmund was the first master.

His Home was a long white-washed building that had been used previously as a dairy. Some inside walls had been put in leaving two rooms with fires for himself and his wife, a long room in the middle as a classroom and dining room for the foundlings, and two rooms at the end, in one of which the boys slept and in the other the girls. At the back there was a pump so that the foundlings could be clean.

The more children there were there, the more Edmund was paid, and the extra money he gained was worth far more than the food that each new child required.

And now here were two more coming, and the letter contained ten pounds.

Edmund read the letter slowly. He had never had much success at school; he had some difficulty in writing to let the trustees know he would be taking in two more children, but little difficulty in pocketing the ten pounds.

48

Captain Matthew Kay had had the most miserable month of his life. He did not know what to do and he had no-one to whom he could safely turn for help.

The Colonel was satisfied that the Captain was on the trail of the smugglers, the innkeeper of the Sloop was satisfied that he was not, and the Magistrate at Newick had even congratulated him on his progress and had several times invited him to drink at his house. Sir Charles Marsh had even provided his men with better accommodation at Newick than the musty barns at the Sloop. Certainly the men were much more contented. Their food and drink was ample; there were less exercises creeping over the slippery chalk of the Downs and avoiding gorse bushes and icy ponds, and more visits to the fellowship of the inn and the beautiful girls of Newick.

Matthew was still at the Sloop suffering the contemptuous service of the innkeeper. He noted but did not investigate the fact that the barns vacated by the soldiers were being filled again. They were usually filled at night when the noise of boats bumping the wooden quay, the low curses of men and the swishing flow of water half wakened him from sleep.

He knew he had discovered a large, active smuggling ring, but he could do nothing. He thought about defying the innkeeper, about resignation from the army, and even about suicide. He couldn't make up his mind.

He sat unhappily in his dark room drinking brandy half-heartedly. The innkeeper was always generous with drink. There was a knock at the door. It did not sound like the innkeeper who usually came in as he knocked. Matthew got up and opened the door.

There stood Eugene Chipperfield. Matthew was surprised. They had talked once at Kilmore House without finding much in common.

110

'Ah, Parson Chipperfield,' he said trying to sound welcoming. 'Come and sit down and have a drink.'

'Thank you, Captain,' replied Eugene. 'I will not drink now.'

He paused and felt the same distaste for the army as he had felt at home with his military father. But then his sense of duty took over.

'I have important news which I felt might help you to track down the smugglers.'

At that moment there was a knock and the door was flung open. In came Samuel Jebb with a jug and tankard on a tray.

'I have brought this for your guest,' he said roughly, and put it noisily on the table.

'Have you come to save the Captain's soul? I think he needs it.'

The innkeeper laughed.

'Thank you, Jebb,' replied Matthew trying to take control. 'You may leave us now.'

The innkeeper had shown no inclination to leave, but with an ill-favoured look at Eugene he did.

Matthew looked curiously at Eugene. He had judged Eugene to be a weak and dull parson. What could he know of real life? Before he spoke he walked to the door and opened it quietly. There was nobody outside. He closed the door and again looked at Eugene who sat nervously at the edge of the chair.

'What do you know of smugglers?' he asked brusquely.

'I meet them all the time,' came the unexpected answer. 'I have discovered that when I visit my poor parishioners, most of them find enough to keep living only by smuggling.'

'And they tell you this?'

'Yes.'

'You will not help your poor parishioners if I arrest them. They will be hanged. You put their lives in jeopardy by your words.'

'That is why I have come to see you. They are not the leaders; they are not those who become rich; they are the poor men used by the evil men. It is the leaders you must find, Captain.'

'I am aware of that, Parson. And have your poor friends told you who the leaders are?'

'A smuggler, Captain, will never give you another name even on the scaffold.'

'I have come to believe that no man or woman in Sussex will murmur one word about the identity of a smuggler,' said the Captain bitterly. 'Perhaps because every one of them is a smuggler.'

Eugene was disappointed at the Captain's reaction, but he was determined to go on.

'I have some news, Captain, that may help to find the leaders. I shall pass it on to you if you will heed my conditions.'

'Your conditions!'

Matthew looked aggressive. Here was a nervous blockhead of a parson daring to make conditions with an officer in His Majesty's Army.

And then a gleam of light flickered into Matthew's dark, uneasy mind. If he captured the leader what did it matter what Jebb said. His mind was still muzzy with brandy, but for the first time his duty was clear again. He stood up, threw open the window and the cold October wind blew in. Matthew knew he was half drunk. He also knew why he had been left at the Sloop.

He turned to talk to the Curate.

49

The last day that Captain Cripps and Richard and Selina had together was a happy one.

Both the children were adventurous; they loved riding and climbing. They chattered endlessly. It was the first time a grown-up had allowed them to or had shown any interest in what they said. Then they left the coast and looked for the Foundlings' Home.

The Captain was disappointed when he found it, and even more disappointed when he talked to the Master, Edmund Shillibeer. He was a man he would have taken as a sailor, but not a man to run the Foundlings' Home. He looked in the barn which served as the children's living room. He saw some twenty children. They did not look hungry, but their faces were expressionless and showed little interest in the arrival of the Captain and the two children.

'You will see, Captain Cripps, they are all well fed, although we get little enough money to pay for the food. My wife has become a slave to these children.'

At this moment Mrs Shillibeer appeared sailing grandly from her room in a fine purple dress, and with ornaments gleaming and with a smiling face white and red from much hard labour in front of the mirror.

The Captain hardly felt that this splendid woman could in any way be called a slave. The children scattered as she approached as rowing boats do when a battleship looms up.

She greeted Richard and Selina with some interest and Captain Cripps with more.

The sad time had come for parting. At the last moment the Captain asked the children for the address of their Aunt Sarah. Selina told him. Captain Cripps trotted back to his ship, and the children turned to face their new life in England.

50

Eugene Chipperfield was glad he had been brave enough to visit Captain Kay. He was not sure how successful the meeting had been. He had been listened to carefully and courteously enough, but Eugene realized that the Captain was already half-drunk. He also knew that he must find more information about the smugglers' activities, for it appeared unlikely that the Captain would.

Winter was coming on. The last leaves had left the oaks and elms. The fields were cold and wet. Eugene was visiting his parishioners with loaves of bread which his wife had baked.

He knocked and entered the house of Arthur Scott. It was a one-roomed cottage with walls mixed with mud and straw, and a beaten mud floor. It was dark because the windows were covered with grey cloth, that had once been the wedding dress of Anne Scott. It was warm because the fire was blazing. Over the fire a large pot was hung and the contents were being stirred by Anne.

Two of her four children were playing with sticks in a wooden tub in the middle of the floor. It was everybody's bath tub. The other two, Eugene learnt, were gathering fuel in the woods.

Eugene was warmly welcomed by Anne and the children. The once beautiful Anne turned a tired wrinkled face to Eugene as she thanked him and then sent the two children down to the Ouse with a bucket for water.

Arthur, Eugene knew, was a reluctant smuggler, just as his father had been. Life had taught him that there was no way in which he could clothe and feed Anne and his four children on seven shillings a week, and so it was that the four shillings he gained from a night's work was welcome indeed.

'They do say,' said Anne to Eugene, 'that early in the new year there'll be one pound for a night's work down at Newhaven. It will be on the night of the new moon.'

She and nearly everyone else in Barcombe regarded this as a right and proper though slightly risky occupation for a husband.

Eugene thanked her and took his bread round to the next cottage of Jonathan Hindley.

51

It was on 1st November 1746 that Sarah received a letter that jerked her out of her pleasant routine of life in Whitechapel.

'Dear Miss Crossman,

I trust you will forgive the impertinence of my writing this letter. Please accept my assurance that its cause is solely the affection I bear to two children, and I write to you in the belief that your affection for the children is greater than mine. The children are your nephew and niece, Richard and Selina Calvert.

I had the privilege of bringing them to Plymouth from Sierra Leone at the request of John Newton, the son of a great friend of mine, in HMS *Harwich*, the ship of which I am captain.

Your brother-in-law and sister wrote in reply to my letter that they felt it unwise to send the children to Sussex. They feared the dangers and difficulties of the roads in winter, though to be sure there was no winter yet in Devon and the coaches ran regularly to Exeter.

Sir Adam arranged for the children to be boarded at a Home for Foundlings in Crown Hill. I took them there yesterday, expecting a place of education run by a scholar and his wife in whom learning and kindness would be equally mixed.

Instead I found a hovel that would not be fit for my cattle, run by a scoundrel, whose counting I suspect does not progress beyond money and a wife who was little more than a saucy trollop.

I trust you will forgive these strong words, but it is these two persons that your nephew and niece are under. Tomorrow I shall be away at sea. The affection to you of Richard and Selina assures me that you will take pains to bring them to you. I enclose a map which some worthy man may use to find them and free them.

Mr Shillibeer, their master, will not give them up easily as each child means money to him. It is not for you to go, but find a man of courage and virtue for the task. I shall communicate again when I return in three months.

I am your most devoted servant,
George Cripps (Captain, Royal Navy)'

Sarah read the letter twice. Her anger grew. Adam and Katharine had not told her the truth. For whatever reason the children were not wanted at Kilmore House. But that was not the main problem. It was up to her to have the children released from Plymouth. She would not disappoint the Captain.

She called for Mrs Collington whose common sense rarely let her down.

'It would not be seemly for you or me to take the children from the home. Indeed if force is needed perhaps we couldn't. We must find an honest Christian man in Plymouth who will face this Shillibeer and bring the children away from him.'

They pondered the problem. Neither of them had ever been to the West Country. They knew nobody in Plymouth.

Suddenly they both looked at one another.

'I know someone who loves the West Country and has many friends there.'

'So do I,' replied Mrs Collington.

'We shall see him when he's next in London,' said Sarah.

52

A few days later two letters were received by Sir Adam. The first was an ill-written one from Edmund Shillibeer saying that the two children had arrived from Africa safely. They were wild little things who had few clothes and they ate very heartily. He wondered if Sir Adam could send some more money so that the kindness of his wife to the children might be rewarded.

Sir Adam was pleased. The children were safely there and there thy would stay and be educated. Not another penny would Edmund Shillibeer get from him. Sir Adam asked Lady Katharine to write to Peggy and tell her the children were being well educated at a school in Plymouth.

Then Sir Adam remembered the second letter.

'There is a letter for you from Peggy,' he said, handing it to her.

Katharine took it and looked at it.

'It is not Peggy's writing,' she remarked. She opened it and began to read. She burst into tears.

'Peggy's dead,' she cried.

Sir Adam seized the letter and read it, as Katharine sat down and sobbed quietly. She had loved Peggy even though she had married so far beneath her.

Her husband read the whole letter.

'The scoundrel!' he muttered. Katharine looked up in surprise.

'Some Captain Clow has written this letter. He is a slave-trader and he says that the Camaranca station is worthless. He has taken it over, but regrets he can send no money for it. The scoundrel!'

'But what happened to Peggy?'

'She died of a fever. Captain Clow claims his wife nursed her, but she was too ill to be saved.'

'Oh Peggy, Peggy,' sobbed Katharine.

Sir Adam looked at the letter. His thoughts about Peggy's death were not the same as Katharine's. He felt he was now absolved from his responsibilities to her children. The money she had sent could now be regarded as Katharine's share of the Camaranca Trading Company. Clearly this Captain Clow was not going to give it to her. He smiled.

Katharine looked up surprised. Sir Adam returned her look.

'I'm glad I've got her children well placed,' he said. 'They will be better in Plymouth than here. I have Sir Charles Marsh's word for that. You must write to Sarah and tell her we have settled Peggy's children at a good school in Plymouth. We don't want her fussing over it all.'

Then seeing his wife sobbing he said, 'Oh, and tell her of Peggy's death, Peggy's sad death.'

53

Richard and Selina had been brought up to accept whatever life brought them without grumbling. However, after a few weeks they were disappointed that all their glorious hopes about life in England were fading in the 'Home for Foundlings'.

The children there were neither friendly nor unfriendly. When they did talk, which was not often, their broad West Country accents baffled Richard and Selina. They were sad children who had been deserted and half starved on the streets. They could hardly remember their mothers and none could remember their fathers. They never laughed.

Richard and Selina soon discovered they were not at school. There were no lessons; neither a book nor a pen were to be seen.

Mr Edmund Shillibeer did not believe in book learning. He had done excellently without it. It cost a lot of money to bring a schoolmaster in. When the trustees of the Home found a schoolmaster and Edmund Shillibeer was informed that he would be required to pay him three shillings a day from his income, he told them that he could teach the children himself. Sir Roger Marsh advised the trustees to agree with this.

Mr Shillibeer's educational principle was to make his boys useful working men, or if they showed no signs of becoming useful he would send them to the navy.

There was an acre of ground behind the Home, which had once grazed some cows for the dairy. Here the boys dug and planted vegetables, collected eggs from hens and apples from the trees, strengthened the hedge that surrounded the ground, and chopped wood.

When the south west wind blew, and it did this often, and blew the slate tiles from the roof of the Home, the boys climbed a perilous ladder they had built, and perched themselves on the sloping slates to fill in the holes.

The girls did get nearer to a school lesson than the boys. Every morning at ten o'clock except on Sunday, a sewing teacher, Miss Pamela Horspool, came to the girls for two hours. She was paid two shillings a week, but she was more worthwhile to Mr Shillibeer, for all the children's clothes were kept in a wearable condition. The children loved her especially as she told them stories as they sewed. She told them of Hercules, of Samson, of Francis Drake, of Robinson Crusoe and of Jesus. She always started her story after every girl knew what she had to do, with 'I am going to tell you a story about another strong man.'

When Miss Horspool left at mid-day, the girls were trained to become useful maids. With the help of Joanna Moore, a sixteen year old girl who lived in a shed attached to the Home and who only cost a shilling a month, the girls learnt to clean, light fires, wash dishes, cook, clear the fires and wait on Mr Shillibeer. The girls loved Joanna too, because she only sounded cross when Mr and Mrs Shillibeer were there. When she woke them at five o'clock in the morning she always made it sound as though it was the start of a lovely day, and when she put them to bed at seven o'clock in the evening, she kissed each one. Their mothers had rarely done that.

Mr Shillibeer did not like children, but he knew that though they caused more trouble than keeping pigs, an occupation he would like to have done, they paid much better. He looked upon them as small, unsatisfactory grown-ups who had to be taught to be useful and obedient.

He quickly came to dislike Richard. On their first morning the boys were told to sit in one corner of their room to await the morning's instructions, Richard had got up, walked across the room to Mr Shillibeer's door which was open. Inside Mr Shillibeer was sitting by a roaring fire eating eggs and bacon.

Richard asked, 'Where are the books, sir?'

Mr Shillibeer, with a mouthful, shouted with difficulty 'What?'

'Where are the books, sir? I want to read.'

Mr Shillibeer could not quite understand the request, but he realized the boy was a trouble-maker. He shouted to Richard to go at once where he should be or he would be punished. Richard went back to the other boys who gazed at him in

121

amazement and admiration. That morning Richard found himself digging, and also that afternoon. He was kept digging longer than the other boys. That was his punishment.

Two weeks later when once again the boys were sitting on the floor awaiting instructions, Richard heard a noise which thrilled him. There were drums. It could be Africa again. And there were fifes playing. And there were marching feet. And there were cheers.

Now there were no windows in their room low enough for the children to see through. The large door at the front was locked. However Richard was observant. He had noticed the planks at the bottom were rotten and the nails which had held them to the door frame had fallen out. He seized a broom, went to the door and pushed the handle between the planks and the frame. He stuck the handle in the ground outside and levered the planks open. There was not much room, but children at the home did not take much space.

'We can get out,' he called. 'Who will come with me?'

No children were allowed out of the Home. Some had spent three years never out of the rooms or the garden at the back. Most of them looked at him in astonishment and sat still but two of them who still had spirit and were becoming his friends, Mark Hedges and Simon Pepler, jumped up and joined him at the door. Richard held the planks back as Mark and Simon slipped through and out, and with more difficulty and with the door wedged slightly open, Richard joined them.

It was exciting. Exciting to be out and to see the world again. Rows of sailors were marching by. Behind them came the fife drum and drum band. And round them trotted magnificent horses ridden by equally magnificent naval officers. Richard looked longingly for Captain Cripps.

Then in the rear came the smart confident Petty Officers smiling on the crowds, who were standing and cheering on both sides of the road.

'A life on the ocean wave,' they shouted. 'And the King's shilling! Come and join us, and say goodbye to your wives.'

There was much laughter and shouting. Richard, Mark and Simon were spellbound. They longed to join the navy.

Edmund Shillibeer took longer than usual over his breakfast that morning, but in the end the excitement outside roused him. He would go and look. He took the key and started to unlock the great door. He found the door handle upside down. He looked at the boys. They were sitting cowering in the corner as usual.

He opened the door and a blast of cheerful music and excitement entered the dull, dark room. But it was not the sailors and band which Edmund Shillibeer saw, but his three boys. He grabbed them roughly and threw them back into the room. They fell on the floor. As they were scrambling up he grabbed them again and led them towards his room.

'Stand there,' he growled. 'Joanna, lock the main door. I am going to beat these boys.'

'Oh, sir. They were only . . . .' pleaded Joanna.

'Be careful I do not beat you too,' shouted the enraged Edmund. 'You are all here to obey. And obey you will.' He entered his room and came back with his rod.

'Come close and watch boys,' he shouted to the others in the corner. 'This is what happens when you disobey me.'

He beat Mark, then Simon, but he kept Richard till last. He gave him two extra strokes. He wanted him to cry and beg forgiveness. Richard didn't do either.

He told the boys to get back to the corner.

He went back to his room and his fire. In spite of his exercise he felt cold. Then he reflected he had not received the extra money he wanted from Sir Adam. He would get Joanna to help him to write again. He was beginning to wish he had not taken these trouble-making children.

54

John Wesley, one of the most organized of men, would always try to fit in a request from Sarah Crossman for a visit. He loved her enthusiasm and her honesty. Not many of the ladies and gentlemen of England had responded to the call of Jesus Christ, but Sarah had, and John looked forward to a further chance to instruct her in the faith.

She offered him a cup of tea which he accepted.

'In July,' he said, 'I began a week's experiment of leaving off tea, but my flesh protested against it. I was but half awake and half alive all day, and my headache so increased towards noon that I could neither speak nor think. It so weakened me that I could hardly sit on my horse. I returned to tea so you can see how gladly I drink this cup.'

'Well, I trust it will help you to think,' said Sarah. 'Mrs Collington and I have prayed about a problem, and I think God has sent you to put it right.'

Then she told him the story of Richard and Selina, and finished by asking whether he had good friends in Plymouth.

'We have a society that I love in Plymouth,' said John, 'and none better than Herbert Jenkins. He has the strength of Samson and the humility of Jesus. When I went to Plymouth some two months ago, a big crowd gathered and Herbert spoke a plain, honest sermon. The crowd faded away, because they wanted to hear me, not him. But Herbert was not offended and still loves me.'

'That sounds just the man,' Sarah put in. 'As strong as Samson. That is good. He can fight the Master of the Foundlings Home and take the children away.'

'No,' replied John. 'Herbert will not fight now; not since he has given his life to Jesus.'

'But he would be fighting a good cause!'

'No, God can work without fighting. I shall let him know about the children, and will call you to help when needed. God's ways are not our ways. You keep praying, Sarah.'

55

Sir Charles Marsh was at Kilmore House. He knew the value of encouragement, and he also knew that Sir Adam was one who needed it continually.

He heard with satisfaction that Edmund Shillibeer, not one of his favourite old soldiers, was doing his duty as far away as Plymouth. Again he heard Adam's worries about Captain Kay and his dragoons remaining so close.

Sir Charles then told him one fact to strengthen his wavering resolve, and one fact that would cheer him.

'You must remember, Adam,' he said, sipping his brandy, 'that your income increasingly relies on free-trading. The foundation for comfort in the enjoyments of this life is the pursuit of the trade that provides the means for it. Thus a Sussex free-trader will abound in wealth, have fine houses, be handsome in his person, have titles of dignity and be above his fellow creatures.

'Is not this an incomparable gain, compared with the worries of a Captain of the Dragoons, who, believe me, Adam, is drinking himself to death at the Sloop. Jebb can be a generous man.'

'You are right, Charles. It is just that I am surrounded by difficulties, and my just expectations of money from my trading companies have vanished.'

'I can cheer you in that also, Adam. On the night of 14th January, the night of the new moon, two French ships will anchor off Newhaven. Their cargo will exceed any that the free-traders of Rye and Arundel have ever had. Every man of yours and mine will be there, every barn and many a church by the Ouse will be full, and for you, Adam there will be one thousand pounds.'

Charles sipped his brandy and looked at Adam. Yes, he had had the right effect.

Adam stood up.

'An ounce of your wit, Charles, is worth a ton of other people's. I and my men will be with you. A fig for the Dragoons.'

56

Eugene Chipperfield felt he had been woken from a long sleep by that one question at the Harvest Supper.

He saw the poor people in his parish in a new way. They were anxious for their families. They needed money to provide enough to feed and clothe them. By starting work at six every morning and working till six in the evening a labourer could not earn enough for this. When illness came they could only use old fashioned remedies. No doctor would come unpaid.

Mrs Collard had rheumatism which half bowed her to the ground and five children under eight years old. No wonder they all looked dirty and half-starved.

The Willis family always seemed ill. Eugene discovered that on most days all they had was bread and milk and the bread was supplied by him.

On a cold November day with icy rain lashing Barcombe, Eugene found the Bull family all curled up on their straw palliasses under old blankets. The children had been too ill to keep warm. The bread Eugene's wife had baked was the first meal they had had.

And yet when it came to Sunday they all tried to look clean and come to church. And the church gave them nothing. As Eugene re-read the Gospels he realized that it was to the Collards, and Willises and Bulls that Jesus went most gladly.

And now Eugene intended to put an end to the smuggling in Barcombe (perhaps Eugene had more of the single-mindedness of his father than he thought). But if he did would his parishioners starve? He had much to think about.

57

Herbert Jenkins of Plymouth was tall and broad. He stood head and shoulders above most of those around him. He had heard John Wesley speaking by Plymouth Sound and had given his life to Jesus. He worked as a carpenter by day and spoke simply to the little society of Methodists in the evenings and on Sundays.

His first letter from John Wesley came as a surprise. He expected instructions for the society, or perhaps a copy of one of Wesley's wonderful sermons. But it was neither. It was about two little children in a place just outside Plymouth.

Herbert prayed about it, took a letter that Wesley had enclosed and laying aside his work for the day marched up to the Home for Foundlings. He banged on the door. Silence reigned. He banged again. He heard the unlocking of the door, which then opened six inches. A nervous girl's face looked through the gap.

'I wish to see Mr Shillibeer,' he said.

'Yes, sir,' came the reply from Joanna.

Herbert could hear the door being locked again. He waited for nearly five minutes musing on various things such as what a strange building it was for a foundlings' home, what a strange greeting he had had, and how it required a proper carpenter to put this damaged door to rights.

The door was opened again and out came Edmund Shillibeer with a suspicious look in his eye. When he saw Herbert he became more friendly. An army man appreciates strength.

'Well?' he said.

'I have a message from Miss Sarah Crossman. She wishes to take her nephew and niece from here.'

Edmund's suspicions returned.

'You have come to the wrong place. No-one called Crossman here.'

'They are called,' and Herbert consulted the letter, 'Richard and Selina Calvert. Here's the letter from Miss Crossman to you.'

Edmund thought quickly. He took the letter and struggled unsuccessfully to read it. He was wondering whether his refusal would bring a fight. Edmund Shillibeer was strong, but he realized that Herbert was stronger. He would be cautious.

'Yes, they are here, but I have orders from Sir Adam Kilmore to keep them.'

He was hoping that Herbert might now produce some money to reinforce the Aunt's claim, but there was no sign of any.

'I believe Miss Crossman has only thoughts for the well-being of the children,' said Herbert mildly.

'That may be,' replied Edmund encouraged by this mildness. 'But I must obey my orders. I am an old soldier. I wish you good day, sir.' With that he opened the door wide behind him, giving Herbert his first view of the Home. There in the dim light he could see the girls on small stalls in the middle of the floor sewing, and there was the voice of someone reading.

The door slammed in front of him. Herbert did not try to stop it. Herbert had recognized that voice inside.

58

'What about this curate of yours?' asked Sir Charles. 'Jebb tells me he has been seeing the Captain, and he thought he heard them talking about smuggling.'

Sir Adam laughed. He felt pleased. For once he knew more than Sir Charles.

'My dear Charles,' he exclaimed, 'you need have no worries about him. He is a dull parson only worried about increasing his money. He has as much chance of worrying the smugglers as the brandy in my glass has of putting out that fire.'

The great log fire blazed heartily as they made final plans for 14th January.

Captain Kay visited Eugene's house for the first time. It was a fine house outside, but inside it was cold and damp. Their only warmth was in the kitchen. A wood fire burned, and the satisfying smell of bread from the bakery hung in the air.

'It is 14th January on the west beach at Newhaven,' said Eugene. 'The men of Barcombe say it will be the biggest load yet.'

Matthew trotted up Scaynes Hill on his way back to the Sloop. He was feeling happier now even though he suspected he might soon be dead in a ditch.

Pamela Horspool was neither beautiful nor rich, which explains the reasons that at thirty-five she was not married. When young she had grieved greatly when she heard the youth of Plymouth say none too quietly, 'She looks like a horse.'

'No,' came the reply, 'Give me a horse any day. A horse is worth some money.'

But her parents had believed in education. Their house had many books and she could translate Latin and French as well as any boy from Eton.

Now she could laugh about looking like a horse. Indeed as she looked in a mirror she could see the likeness. But Pamela had a purpose in life since she like Herbert had heard John Wesley preach by the Sound. She thrilled when Herbert came and talked to her about Richard and Selina. It might mean the loss of two shillings a week and the search for other work, but she was still thrilled. Following Jesus was for her doing not saying.

She wrote a little note, put it in her book as she put on her coat and prepared for a frosty walk to the Foundlings' Home on the first day of December in 1746. One of the reasons for her job there was Mrs Shillibeer, a vain but not unkind woman. Pamela's sewing was superb, and she passed this skill on to many of the girls. Mrs Shillibeer's sewing was not superb. Thus when she wanted lace added to her dress, or changes made to her many suits of clothes, who better than Pamela and the girls?

That morning as they sat in the middle of the room sewing, Pamela slipped her note to Selina and said quietly, 'Give it to Richard, when he comes in.'

Selina hid the note in her dirty white dress, knowing it would not be easy. The girls were kept strictly apart from the boys. It was one of her greatest griefs she could never talk to Richard. The boys were in the garden at present but in an hour's time would come in and sit in the corner of the room and wait for their drink of milk and hunk of bread. The girls would wait in the opposite corner.

As the boys wandered in and listlessly sat down, Mrs Shillibeer came out to look at how the lace fitted the collar of her scarlet dress. Pamela showed it to her. She was pleased, but out of the corner of her eye she caught sight of Selina creeping towards the boys.

'Come back girl,' Mrs Shillibeer shouted. She didn't know the names of any of them but she knew the rules.

Selina stopped, but she had caught Richard's eye. She dropped her paper and rejoined the other girls. Richard had seen it. Mrs Shillibeer had lost interest and was holding up her dress to the light. Richard's hand slid towards the paper and grabbed it.

Pamela was pleased. Mr Shillibeer did not seem to be

around. Perhaps it was a credit to his efficiency that the Home moved as quietly and obediently and miserably without him as with him.

A well-pleased Mrs Shillibeer returned to her fire and the slices of ham that Joanna had prepared for her. Pamela stood up to go. Her coat had not been taken off for the room was usually as cold as it was outside. She asked Joanna to open the door. Joanna fetched the key and opened it wide. The rays of the sun beamed warmth and light in, as Pamela Horspool and two small children went out.

'Close to me, dears,' said Pamela. The brave Joanna shut and locked the door. No-one in the room, dim again, said a thing.

Edmund Shillibeer was returning with his wagon from a visit to the farmers near the moor to find where he could buy the cheapest oats. He had been successful and was pleased at how little the porridge which was the children's staple food had cost him.

As he turned the corner, he saw the ugly Miss Horspool coming out and turning towards Plymouth. Just as he was pulling his horse into the yard he caught sight of a small figure by Miss Horspool. It looked like a boy; it looked like Richard Calvert. Hastily he tied the horse in the yard, and rushed through the back door into his kitchen. His wife was sitting happily eating. He hurried into the main room. Joanna was handing out mugs of milk to the boys. The girls were sitting waiting for theirs. He strode over and looked at the boys.

'Where is Richard Calvert?' he stormed.

There was no reply – only blank stares.

'Bring me the key,' he shouted to Joanna.

'Richard is in the garden,' Mark piped up.

'Working in the garden,' Simon said. They were to be beaten for this later, but the lies served their purpose. Edmund rushed into the garden. He couldn't believe Richard had got away, and it was indeed possible that Richard had not finished his morning task and was still working at it. But Richard wasn't there. He hurried back in and found that Selina was also missing. Without another word (he would have plenty to say later) he went back to the wagon, pushed off the sacks of oats, and urged his tired horse out of the yard. Across the road stood two of Edmund's drinking cronies in front of 'The Six

Bells'.

'Come here, Jim and Job, I have some money for you.'

Still holding their tankards they ran across the road and jumped into the wagon. They had heard the magic word 'money'. Sir Adam will pay heavily for this, thought Edmund grimly.

'Two children have escaped with that hag Horspool. We must get them. I know where she lives!' He whipped his horse, and the trio trotted in pursuit.

59

A man stood on the cliffs west of Newhaven. It was a desolate place. The cliffs white and brown fell some sixty feet down to the stony beach. Beside him gorse bushes and rough grass stretched westwards. To his left the path went gently lower to the fishing village of Newhaven.

He looked out over the grey sea towards France. There was not a boat to be seen. The waves ceaselessly turned over the rounded stones and then sadly retreated with a hiss. The man admired the power of the sea, but he felt its sadness too.

The man was Eugene Chipperfield who had borrowed a horse from farmer Cornwell and had ridden through Lewes to have his first look at Newhaven.

The man who should have been there, was sitting in the Sloop Inn drinking brandy. He was a man who could not make up his mind.

60

Miss Horspool had something of the spirit of Miss Crossman in her. She was not afraid of anyone, least of all Mr Shillibeer, and she loved action. But there was not much chance of action for women in 1746. Their duty was the humble round, the common task. Thus the meeting with Herbert Jenkins was a great day for Pamela.

Pamela did not particularly like men. The heartfelt memories of their rudeness while she was young had had a lasting effect. However, first the coming of John Wesley and second the encouragement of Herbert Jenkins had placed these two men rather higher than others in her esteem.

Her dreams of action had come true. She was playing a part in an escape. Pursuers would soon be after them. She was not afraid, nor to her relief were the children. They had obeyed instructions and had managed the most difficult part of getting out of the Home half hidden under her coat perfectly. They now trotted briskly beside her clinging on to her hands. The observant Richard, caught a quick glimpse of the return of Edmund Shillibeer.

'Beery's back,' he gasped, using the nickname he had learnt from Mark and Simon.

'Then he will soon be after us. A little faster, children.'

The road ran straight for a mile towards Plymouth. There help awaited them. A small wagon and Herbert Jenkins would be waiting in an inn yard. Pamela's happy thoughts of a race won and the children safe were suddenly broken by a rough shout from a voice they knew well.

'There they are. We will have them, the brats.' Pamela, Richard and Selina looked round, and their hearts sank. In full view was Edmund and his two friends standing at the front of the wagon and waving at them with sticks. Pamela knew there were only four hundred yards to go, but she also knew that they would be caught before they had got half-way.

The people of Plymouth were standing watching the strange sight of the running woman, the two dirty children and the pursuing wagon with its shouting men.

Pamela did not hesitate. Rows of cottages stood on either side of the road. She saw one with an open door, and dashing through it pulled the children beside her. The children fell on the floor panting, while Pamela supported herself against a large table she had run into. She found herself staring in the grim face of a large woman.

'May we stay here?' she asked breathlessly. 'Bad men are trying to capture these children.'

As soon as she spoke the expression on the woman's face changed. Pamela spoke with a Plymouth accent.

'Hide under the table,' she said. Pamela bent down and crawled under. The other two scuttled in beside her. Over the table their protector put a great blanket which reached the floor.

'Ugh,' murmured Selina in the dark, stuffiness.

'Hide and seek,' said Pamela. 'Be quiet.'

In what seemed only a few seconds, the three could hear the muffled shouts of men outside.

'They are in one of these houses,' shouted Edmund. 'Did you see a woman and two children enter a house?' he asked a gathering crowd.

He did not speak in a Plymouth accent. They did not answer.

'You must have seen them,' he shouted angrily. 'This is a magistrate's matter, you know.'

The crowd did not answer. Drink had not lessened the eyesight of Job.

'They went in one of these,' he said, pointing correctly to the cottage the trio were in and the one next door.

Edmund looked. The house they were in now had a closed door, the other one's door was open. He reckoned his prey were probably behind a closed door. He approached it with his allies. A large woman stood in front of the door, 'I wish to go in, Madam,' he said as politely as he could.

'No-one enters my house without permission,' came the reply. 'And I give no permission.'

Jim looked at Edmund, who was not used to women

standing up to him. Edmund was quite prepared to throw the woman aside, but his army training had taught him to sum up the opposition first. He was conscious that the crowd growing round him was not on his side. There were growing shouts from the crowd. Edmund tried again to make the woman let him pass, when suddenly a louder shout won silence.

'Shillibeer,' a voice bellowed.

Edmund looked round. There in the middle of the road was Herbert Jenkins. In a flash Edmund realized who was at the heart of all the trouble. It was Jenkins who was kidnapping his children.

'Come back,' he said to Jim and Job, 'this is the man who has got them.' They hesitated and then hurried towards him, but to the disappointment of the crowd, Herbert Jenkins turned round and began to run back down the road. The three were after him.

They found him standing in the innyard in front of his horse and wagon. His wagon was covered by taut sacking.

'They're in there,' shouted Edmund. 'Come on, we have caught them now.'

61

Eugene walked down from the cliff to Newhaven. His next port of call was the small Customs House in the village. There he found the Chief Excise Officer playing cards with his junior officers.

They were surprised to have a visit from a parson. They were more surprised and alarmed at what he had to say.

'We live dangerous lives, Parson,' said the Excise Officer truly enough. He went on to say that they knew all what the parson had told them and perhaps it was true. He then said he would be in touch with the dragoons and finally suggested Eugene stuck to his prayers and left the danger to the Excise Officers.

Eugene was sent on his way, without even the offer of a drink, of which the Customs Officers seemed to have a plentiful supply.

He trotted back to Barcombe thoughtfully.

62

This was the moment Jim and Job had been waiting for. Drink gives you courage, and both were proud fighters without it. It is true that Herbert Jenkins was rather larger and stronger looking than the woman that they had been chasing, but they realized that though large he was obviously a coward and would only fight if he was cornered, and also that there were two of them.

'Give me back my children,' said Edmund fiercely, 'and we'll leave you unharmed.'

Herbert did not reply.

'Go and take the sacking off and get the children,' ordered Edmund. Herbert stretched out his arm in front of them as they walked to the wagon.

'No,' he said firmly.

Jim turned and drove his fist at Herbert's middle. Herbert's arm came down and deflected the blow. Then Herbert's other arm hit Jim's face. Jim fell over backwards and landed in the mud. The spectators who had followed the race down the street cheered. Jim sat up, dazed.

'Now Job, get those children.' Job made a more circuitous journey towards the wagon. Herbert strode across just before Job touched the sacking.

'No,' he said.

Job appeared to turn away, but he was a famous fighter which Edmund, and many of the spectators but not Herbert knew. Then Job sprung round and hit Herbert two hard blows, the first on his face and the second much lower down.

Now there was ignorance on both sides. For Job did not know that Herbert, before he had heard Mr Wesley by the Sound and vowed never to fight again, had been in his youth a great fighter. He had had many fights in the innyard. The second blow made him stoop, but before Job could deliver a third, a mighty fist met his face, and Job found himself sitting next to Jim.

'I said no,' said Herbert.

He took his horse and started to walk away. Edmund Shillibeer felt his prey was escaping, but decided not to fight. He rallied his forlorn troops and told them all they had to do was to stay with him while he followed the wagon at a distance.

Meanwhile, Pamela, Richard and Selina were crouching stifled under the table. Selina was desperate to sneeze and Richard thought he was suffocating, but a gesture from Pamela kept them quiet. Then, at last, their protector pulled off the blanket and said, 'They have gone,' and she pointed down the road where cheers could be heard.

'The King's Head?' asked Pamela. 'But not down the road.'

Their protector took them between two cottages, and pointed across the field. They said goodbye.

Holding Pamela's hand, Selina and Richard ploughed through a muddy field, slipping and sliding but never stopping. Selina lost a shoe as her foot sank in the mud, but she said nothing. They reached a rough stony path, which cut Selina's feet but still she said nothing. Then a road, and another road and then the King's Head.

Pamela gave a cry of delight.

'We are there, children. Here is the coach that will take you to your Aunt.' They looked with wonder at the great red stage coach. Selina, forgetting her wounds, said, 'It's a house on wheels.' Six horses were harnessed in front held in by wooden poles.

Pamela had not expected to see the children on to the coach. That had been Herbert's duty. However, she was confident that the arrangements had been made. She knew that the stage coach left at two o'clock and that their places had been bought to Exeter. The coachman was already perched in his seat which projected from the front. He was dressed in a magnificent red coat with a black tricorne hat. He showed no interest in the passengers.

Down below was his guard. His duty appeared to be to help the passengers in. There was room for six in two sets of seats facing one another. Attached behind the coach was a huge wicker basket to contain luggage.

As they stood by the door the guard was helping a large lady

141

into the cab. His way of helping was to shove her huge backside through the narrow door into the darkness. As he did it he winked at those standing round suggesting the coach was now full.

Pamela approached him.

'These two children have places for Exeter,' she said.

The guard was in a merry mood. 'Are you Mr Jenkins?' he asked in a loud voice so that the crowd might hear.

Pamela was not amused.

'These two children are from Mr Jenkins.'

'What is your name?' the guard asked Richard.

'Richard Calvert.'

'It seems he doesn't know his father, madam. I am afraid we've no place for them.'

Pamela was just about to try to push them in inspite of the guard, when Herbert Jenkins ran up beside the coach. There was an apologetic guard, a quick goodbye, the crack of a whip and slowly the stage coach lumbered out of the yard. Richard and Selina had been pushed in last. Richard was stuck by the window. He turned to wave goodbye and then had a lovely sight.

Edmund Shillibeer and the battered Jim and Job came running up the road towards the stage coach. Edmund could see Richard and swore loudly, shaking his fist. Richard smiled as the coach turned and he had his last sight of Beery.

'Sit down, sit down,' said the fat lady.

'I cannot see where to sit,' said Selina. The fat lady grabbed her and pushed her to a small space in the middle while she took the seat by the window. Richard squeezed in beside Selina. It was clear that the guard had sold more tickets than there were places.

'What dirty children,' said the fat lady. She was right.

63

Sir Adam Kilmore was a happy man. His crest had been made by a stonemason in Lewes, and now painted in red, gold and green it outshone any Sir Adam could remember in Sussex.

His income was now greater than when the Kilmore Trading Company had been at its prime. He could send George away to school, he would occasionally send some money to his nephew and niece, and when spring came he and his wife would give the largest party Sussex had known. The Duke of Newcastle himself would be invited. Perhaps I might become a Whig, he thought. A life in politics appealed to him. He would mention to the Duke he might be interested in a seat in Lewes.

He strode out of his front door for the third time that December morning. The winter's sun sparkled on his crest. *Pensez à Moi*, he read. He strode proudly back into Kilmore House.

64

The wonder and excitement of the escape for some minutes kept Richard and Selina from realizing their discomfort. Richard had wriggled his way under Selina who was now a blanket over him that stopped him seeing or moving. The bulk of the lady on his left pushed him towards his neighbour on the right. He was a silent, bony man in black and white who appeared to have the worries of the world on him. He did not seem to be aware of his surroundings apart from suddenly swinging his right hand over and trying to push Richard back towards the lady. His hand hurt Richard. As he and Selina were moved into the fatness beside them partly by the silent man and partly by the lurch on the road, Selina received a sharp slap on the side of her face. The angry lady followed this up with, 'You dirty, dirty girl. Go away.'

Selina rubbed her red cheek. She couldn't go away and she didn't cry. Richard's bottom received a terrible beating from the thinly cushioned wooden seat below him. He didn't cry either, but both children began to long for the end of the journey, and they had travelled only two miles.

Selina could see one of the four great wheels which rose the height of the small window in the door. She saw mud, thrown off the wheels as the carriage groaned and creaked its way up the muddy track out of Plymouth. To Richard it seemed like being on board ship again lurching its way through heavy seas.

With a sudden tug the coach stopped. Men's shouts could be heard. The fat lady sat forward digging her elbow into Selina.

'It's cut-throats after our money,' she screamed shrilly.

The silent gentleman looked out of his window. The voices were on his side. He did not say anything.

'They will take my jewels and my money,' she cried crossly. 'Are you not going to save us?'

This last request or rather demand was directed at the silent man. This stirred him into speech.

'Not a cut-throat, Madam,' he muttered.

They all listened as they heard the coachman climbing down from his perch with thumps against the body work. The fat lady sat back, half smothering Richard again, and was only partially reassured by the silent man's outburst of speech.

'He will stick his sword through the coachman, I'll warrant,' she said. 'And then he will murder us.'

The coachman appeared to Selina's sight with his back to the carriage door. A fierce argument started about the price of the fare to Exeter. There was a clink of metal, but it was of money, not a sword. The coachman stood back and opened the door. He looked in, and so did the hopeful passenger.

'You may ride in the basket,' said the coachman. 'I told you the coach is full.'

Three respectable ladies, sisters perhaps, sat on the row opposite Richard and Selina, as unmoved and disapproving and silent as the man opposite. The hopeful passenger was large, covered by a great coat and probably, from his smell, a farmer. He looked at the possibilities. There was a quieter conversation outside and a further clink of money. The door opened again. The farmer stood on the step the coachman fetched for him. He put a strong right arm into the semi-darkness, seized Selina by the top of her arm, wrenched her from Richard, retreated through the door with Selina in the air and dropped her on the ground.

'And this little brat too,' he muttered grabbing Richard who was trying to stand up.

He tugged him from under the fat lady, dragged him over the knees of the silent gentleman, and dumped him on the ground beside his sobbing sister. He sprang up to see the rear end of the farmer disappearing into the coach. There were loud protests from the fat lady as the farmer tried to sit down.

'Those poor little children,' she cried. Two dirty children were preferable to a smelly and clearly drunk farmer. The coachman slammed the door with force.

'Our fares have been paid,' shouted Richard.

'So has his,' smiled the coachman, patting his pocket. 'I won't leave you here. Get in there,' he pointed at the large basket behind.

Richard pulled Selina up.

145

'Get in,' he said.

'I can't,' wept Selina.

The coachman grabbed Selina and dropped her in. She landed on a wooden box. Richard scrambled in beside her. The coachman disappeared and clambered back to his perch.

'It is better here,' shouted Richard, as the whip cracked and the coach slowly rumbled off. 'Hold on tightly to the side.'

Selina was still sobbing on the bottom of the basket with an iron-nailed wooden box bouncing on the side of her and a large leather box swaying on the other. Richard saw the danger. He pulled her up.

'I'll sit on one box, he yelled. 'You on the other.'

Selina tried to, but the motion of the coach made it difficult and painful as they were thrown about. They soon discovered that when the coach went up hill all was well, but as soon as it reached the top and started down, the boxes began to dance around them, so their legs were covered in bruises and cuts.

Selina wept and wept. If Richard had not been there, it would have been her idea of hell. In one of Richard's best moments in his life he tried to cheer her up.

'It is much better here,' he shouted. 'Think of what happened inside when that fat man sat next to that fat lady.'

Selina smiled, and clung to the basket.

65

Sarah and Mrs Collington arrived in Exeter after four hard days on the coach. They had been advised by friends not to trust themselves to the coach at all and if they did, not to go beyond Bath. They ignored both kindly warnings, and though rather battered and tired they were glad they had done so. A purpose makes an uncomfortable journey bearable.

They spent the night at the inn where the Plymouth coach would arrive in the afternoon. The innkeeper and the ostler had no hopes of it arriving on time. In fact the innkeeper appeared to doubt that it would arrive at all. He had many startling stories of disasters on the Devon moors. The ostler added his doubts about the horses which might have managed if the road had not thawed, but he could see an extra day and night on the road in the rain and mud.

The rain splattered the window of the inn and the afternoon seemed long to Sarah and Mrs Collington who half-heartedly played cards and looked at the grey clouds sweeping up from the west. Twilight came early and it was dark before Sarah heard the ostler shout, 'The Plymouth coach, the Plymouth coach,' as he hurried to round up the six horses for the return journey.

Sarah stood under the porch by the front door and peered down the road. She heard a rumble, before she saw two lanterns flickering. The coach lumbered to a juddering stop by the inn. The well-wrapped coachman climbed down from his perch, took the lantern hanging on the side and opened the door. The ostler pushed the steps under it. Out tumbled the silent man, followed by the noisy farmer. There was a pause. The fat lady was determined to be third, reached the door, but had some trouble with her exit as the three ladies left in their seats, were too polite to help from behind.

The fierce words that followed when all were successfully out suggested that they had not been the happiest of travelling companions. The innkeeper was offering them the hospitality of his inn. The ostler was chatting with the coachman. Sarah ran to him and said, 'Where are the children?' He went on talking, but pointed behind the coach.

Sarah saw two people arguing by a big basket. One was a fat lady, and the other a gentleman who looked like a lawyer in black.

'There are two dirty children on my case,' screamed the fat lady at the coachman. The coachman showed little interest but Sarah did. She and Mrs Collington looked over the side of the basket. They saw there Richard and Selina half asleep lying on the boxes, wedged at one side of the basket.

'Richard, Selina,' called Sarah. 'Stand up. I'm your aunt.'

Richard thought it was a dream, and tried to stand. Selina fuzzy with sleep thought perhaps she was dead. Richard pulled her up. Mrs Collington grabbed her and lifted her from the basket, and Sarah helped Richard to clamber out.

Selina was carried into the inn, and Richard stumbled along clinging to Sarah's hand. As they stumbled, drenched, into the inn and climbed to their Aunt's room not a word was said, but Richard knew he was not dreaming and Selina knew she was not dead.

'Tell the innkeeper to bring up a warm bath at once,' Sarah said to Mrs Collington, who hurried downstairs and found an innkeeper delighted to find his guests of last night were staying and that two extra ones had arrived. In two minutes a large wooden tub and three maids with jugs of water arrived upstairs.

The children had taken off their torn, dirty and smelly clothes and were standing by the fire warm and happy. As they talked Sarah saw they were bruised and cut as well as dirty, but decided their spirits were so high that a bath not a doctor would be the finest cure.

☆   ☆   ☆

The news from Sarah that she had Richard and Selina safe in Whitechapel arrived at Kilmore House. The conscience of Katharine, and perhaps of Sir Adam, (though more likely it was the knowledge that he now had plenty of money) meant that the Kilmores were happy enough with the news. Sarah had gone on to say that she would be bringing her nephew and niece to Kilmore House at Christmas and that she had a plan that she thought Adam and Katharine would agree with.

George was also happy with the prospect of his cousins' arrival. He was lonely. He was not allowed to meet any of the farm labourer's children. The curate's children were too young and Sir Roger's children were too old. He knew he was a young gentleman, and could only mix with other young gentlemen. When he first heard that his cousins were in Whitechapel he feared he would not meet them. His father had once told him that owing to an unwise marriage his cousins were not the sort of people he should meet. But something had changed. Apparently Richard was now a gentleman and Selina a lady.

Eugene was also pleased. Perhaps he now would have two more pupils and more money. However Eugene's mind was more concerned with other things that Christmas.

66

Katharine sent a friendly note to Sarah, in which she looked forward to meeting her nephew and niece. She added the news that the Rector of Barcombe, John Blackman, would be with them too, as though this were icing on the cake.

She still worried slightly over the smuggling, but seeing Adam happy was some consolation. She had attempted to get him to tell her the whole story. He implied that though free-trading might not please the King, even so, the local magistrate, the gentlemen of Sussex and the Duke of Newcastle saw it in a different light.

Sarah waited till she knew Richard and Selina better before she told them the news of their mother's death. Selina and Sarah cried together for they had both loved her. To Richard his days in Camaranca seemed long ago, but the news upset him too. His mother had been all that was secure in life.

Nevertheless, Richard and Selina were finding a new security in their Aunt Sarah, who was definite in her opinions like their mother, but who laughed much more.

'You laugh much more than Mother did,' said Selina.

Sarah was not sure whether this was praise or blame, but she replied, 'Your Mother had a hard life.' The children thinking back agreed.

On 23rd December Sarah and her nephew and niece travelled south in a private coach.

'We three,' Sarah announced to the children as they boarded their coach, 'have had enough of stage coaches to last a lifetime. The roads of Sussex are worse than the roads of Devon, and so we shall have two fine horses and a carriage fit for a king.'

Thus they arrived expensively and safely at Kilmore House.

67

Sir Charles and Sir Adam discussed the plans for the landing at Newhaven. Neither of them would be there but Jebb would be in charge of operations, and their labourers would all be there to provide horses and wagons and to be the carriers. Every barn, cellar and garden house in the Ouse valley was empty. So too were the crypts of some churches. Sir Charles, however, felt in view of what Jebb had said it was unwise to ask Eugene Chipperfield, and so St Mary's Church in Barcombe would not be used.

Sir Adam protested only once.

'The Customs should arrest some men,' said Sir Charles. 'I want them to be yours. This will mean they come before me as magistrate and so they will be quite safe.'

'Then it will be more difficult for me to use them in the future.'

'No, Adam. Not when they find how safe they are. I might even help them with a pound or two each. We must retain the good will of the Customs Officers. I have paid much for them. I want all your men to wear a white scarf in their belts. This will give the Customs Officers their targets.'

'But how do I explain this to my men?' asked Adam.

'It is easy enough. Explain that our landers must know to whom to pass the goods.'

'What about the Riding Officer?' asked Adam but received no reply for at that moment there was an unheard of thing at Kilmore House; shouts and screams just outside the door. Adam strode to the door and opened it. He saw George and Richard rolling on the hall floor fighting and Selina shouting at them.

'Go at once to the schoolroom,' he shouted. 'I shall see you later.'

He had no intention of doing so, but it sounded impressive.

He closed the door.

'The Curate is teaching my nephew and niece as well as George. I will have a strong word with him.'

'As long as he goes on teaching, all will be well,' smiled Sir Charles as he prepared to depart.

The fight between Richard and George was a friendly one. They liked each other.

'You're my best friend,' said Richard to George.

'What about Selina?' asked George, pleased but wanting no rivals.

'She's a girl,' said Richard, as though that dealt with the matter finally.

They returned to the schoolroom and to the Curate, who they discovered was a good teacher. They loved their lessons. He started teaching them Latin and Richard worked very hard as he found Selina was as good as he ws. George had already started and enjoyed being the expert. In the Mathematics and English, Richard and Selina found they had been well taught by their mother.

For the last half hour together every day the Curate told them stories about Sussex and smugglers. He told them how good men had been killed all because of smugglers' greed. He told them that smugglers still worked in the Ouse valley. Finally he told them that one night he would take them to the coast and they would see the smugglers in action. He hoped too they would see the villains caught.

'We shall go to watch and learn,' he said. 'We shall go in secret.' George, Richard and Selina all agreed that it should be secret. When they discussed it afterwards, they were all amazed that this serious Curate was going to lead them on this daring adventure.

Perhaps even Eugene Chipperfield himself was amazed, but he felt so strongly about the poverty of the labourers and the risks they had to take to earn enough to look after their families, and the breaking of the law, that he longed to see the organizers caught. A word from Captain Kay had suggested Jebb might be the leader. If Eugene could be sure of this he would inform Sir Charles Marsh. Eugene's problem was how to look after his parishioners if they could no longer smuggle. However, he was beginning to have ideas about this. He had read a large notice in Lewes headed 'Smuggling Acts'. At the end was 'A reward of five hundred pounds will be given for apprehending any offender; a person wounded in apprehending one offender to have fifty pounds extra, and the executors of a person killed to have one hundred pounds.

☆   ☆   ☆

14th January 1747 was a cold day. The roads were ice hard and rutted. ('Better than mud,' said Sir Charles). The villagers of Barcombe were cold and hungry. The Curate of Barcombe made his seven o'clock round with bread and met the children looking for wood. Over their dirty smocks their mothers had tied sacking. After delivering his last loaf of bread to the Scott family Eugene nodded to Arthur, and between them they attached Arthur's most precious possession, his two wheeled wagon to Eugene's horse. Eugene guided his horse to Kilmore House. The lessons that day were less of Latin and more of strict instructions for obedience that night.

Richard and Selina were used to obedience, George less so. The day before Aunt Sarah had departed for Whitechapel in the same hire coach with Parson John Blackman as companion.

'It is like saying goodbye to mother again,' said Richard.

'I think it is worse,' replied Sarah.

Lady Katharine was worried about the tension she saw in Sir Adam again, so that she gave permission without thinking for the Curate to take the three children out that afternoon.

He took them first to the Rectory where they had tea and met Mrs Felicity Chipperfield and the little Chipperfields. Then in the twilight they were off again in the wagon heading for Lewes.

'It's a hard wagon, and a rough road,' complained George. 'We should have ridden on our horses. I have a fine horse, Darkie.'

'But the rest of us haven't, as you know,' replied Eugene sharply. 'Farmer Cornwell has kindly lent us this one.'

'You haven't travelled on the Exeter coach. That was far worse,' said Richard trying to keep up with George.

'I have still got bruises from it,' put in Selina trying to help.

Captain Kay was leaving the Sloop. His supply of drink had been cut off that day. The innkeeper had left early in the morning. The Captain realized he must collect his men from their comfortable retreat at Newick, and take them down to the coast. Colonel Sear had asked for a report on his plans to 'apprehend those guilty of smuggling offences.' The Captain realized that his happy drinking at the Sloop, and his soldiers enjoying the country food and charming female company at Newick did not altogether provide a satisfactory answer.

After midday there was not much work on the Barcombe farms. Labourers, horses and wagons were away travelling south by various routes.

The Customs Officers were all alert at Newhaven. The Chief gave his detailed commands to each member, and showed them all a square of white cloth.

Darkness fell after six o'clock. Stars and the new moon gave a dim, silvery light. Over the horizon from Newhaven the black sails and masts of two ships could be seen.

☆　　☆　　☆

'Look. There are the ships,' said George quietly as they knelt behind the gorse bushes on Newhaven cliff. Eugene was almost relieved when he saw them. This was clearly no wild goose chase.

Below the cliffs the stony beach was empty.

'I can hear men's voices,' whispered Selina, 'but I can't see anyone.'

'You will soon,' answered Eugene, and just after he spoke a man could be seen on the beach. The tide was coming in and so were the ships. From the nearest ship a blue light flashed and then flashed again. The man on the beach struck a flint he was holding with a steel. The sparks flew up. He did it again. There was a grinding sound above the moaning of the sea as both ships dropped anchor less than a quarter of a mile off shore.

Suddenly it seemed to the watchers the beach was full of men. Some were dragging boats down the sloping stones to the sea, some were leading horses and wagons on to the beach and some with lanterns were giving orders in low voices.

Eugene then realized his secret watching point was no longer secret. The people of Newhaven were climbing the gentle path up the cliff as well as thronging the beach.

'Stand up,' said Eugene, 'but stay here. Look, there are the

landers walking out to the ship.'

Men were wading through the waves which some times reached their chests. Others were rowing out. Eugene reckoned there were now more than a hundred people on the part of the beach he could see and there were many more clambering on the cliff. He admired the discipline and efficiency of the whole operation. Everybody seemed to know what to do. Barrels were dropped in the boats. The landers in a cold wet chain that stretched from the ships to the shore passed the boxes and bales from one to another above their heads. At once the carriers were there lifting the loads into the wagons, or balancing them over the horses' backs.

Eugene heard a voice that he recognized raised in command. He looked closely. A lantern flashed in the face of the man as he looked in shore. It was Samuel Jebb.

George too was looking with interest at the man below. There was more light round the piles of goods, and as the next wagon approached, George turned and said to Eugene, 'There's father's men. There with white bands on. They are all villainous smugglers.'

'No; they are just poor men,' said Eugene. 'Talk quietly, George.' It was now clear that the people of Newhaven around them all supported the smugglers.

'Where, oh where are the Customs Men and the Dragoons?' thought Eugene. He looked hopefully around, but could see no-one trying to stop the smugglers. Then he saw two more faces he knew well, the Vicar and the Curate of Newhaven. They picked their way daintily across the pebbles to where Jebb was standing.

'At last,' thought Eugene, 'the church is taking action against this wickedness.'

He saw the parsons talking with Jebb. Jebb gave a command. Two small barrels were taken from the pile. One was handed to the Vicar, and the other to the Curate. They accepted them silently and walked back towards Newhaven considerably less daintily.

Eugene felt sickened. He looked around again for the Customs Men and the Dragoons. He appreciated that they had to wait until the criminals were all fully involved in the operation, but he felt it was now the perfect time. His plan had been to watch the operation and then to support the Dragoons and the Customs Men when the criminals appeared before the magistrates. He thought quickly.

He said to the children firmly, 'Stay here. I shall be back soon.' They were watching as the Barcombe men were piling their wagons high.

Eugene hurried down the path among the people of Newhaven, and turned right onto the beach under the cliff. He stumbled towards Jebb and then shouted in a loud voice, 'Stop, Jebb, in the name of the law.'

There was a moment of silence. Then a large hand clubbed Eugene to the ground. His head hit the stones with a crack, and he found himself looking up at a musket in his face. A strong, hard man turned and looked towards Jebb.

'Do I fire?' he shouted.

Jebb walked over and looked at Eugene, conscious though half-stunned.

'The orders are no blood,' he said. 'Knock him out, put him in a boat and give him to the Frenchies.'

Now Eugene's shout had been a loud one, and it was recognized by others apart from the children on the cliff. Captain Matthew Kay was having a miserable time. He had brought his reluctant and, he discovered half-drunk men to Newhaven with much difficulty. He had had to avoid the roads after Lewes, because he would clearly have been seen and so the Captain had ridden and the men had stumbled over the downs. They had slipped through dark Newhaven and were now squatting under a jetty that provided a harbour. It was some half mile from the action, and gave little view and wet feet as the tide came in. The Captain realized too that the Ouse would soon be full of boats carrying the smuggled goods inland. A lantern on a boat would quickly pick them out. He was pondering means of retreat when he heard Eugene's shout. Indecision flooded him again. He liked Eugene; now he admired him, but to help him would merely mean death on the beach for him and all his men.

The Customs House Chief further up the cliff had also heard the shout. One of his men had been keeping a good look-out and clearly intervention too early would be dangerous. However, the men he was going to arrest had now been spotted and they were now filling their wagons. The Chief decided to make his arrest as they left the beach and were in the middle of

Newhaven. Never before had he seen such a large operation. He did not like other people demanding law and order but he knew that this man was nothing but an interfering curate. He wondered whether he should make his arrests earlier.

Richard, George and Selina saw it all.

'We must go and help him,' cried Selina.

'Stay here,' said Richard, grabbing her to make sure she didn't run off.

'Richard is right,' said George.

Eugene was grabbed by his legs and pulled towards the sea. There was no boat on the shore then, so his captor stood with his foot on Eugene's chest. Eugene did not move, but he did pray.

The operation was by now nearing its end. Jebb was pleased. There would indeed be riches for him. He would willingly have killed Eugene who knew who he was, but his orders had been made clear, and Sir Charles was not a man to defy. Let him be sent to France; he would probably never return. He moved up the beach to the cliffs, and signalled to the Customs look-out man. He passed the signal to his chief.

While he was there the Barcombe carriers had finished loading and the Lindfield labourers moved in.

The Barcombe men started to move their wagons away.

'You know who that was,' said Ebenezer Collard.

'Yes,' muttered Hugh Lines.

'Do we leave him there?'

There was a pause.

'No,' said Thomas Willis. 'We shall take him back to Barcombe. Come with me.'

Robert Lockwood, Daniel Bull and Arthur Scott joined Ebenezer and Thomas. They looked as though they were part of the operation. Robert clubbed the hard man on the back of the head. He fell down beside Eugene with his foot still on his chest. Daniel and Arthur pulled Eugene free, carried him up the beach and dumped him in the cart with the brandy.

'Gee up,' said Thomas. The stumbling horses were glad when they were clear of the beach. They trotted into Newhaven.

No-one had noticed Eugene's escape. Jebb saw the unconscious body lying by the sea, and shouted, 'Get it in the boat.'

One of the French ship's boats had just unloaded its last

cargo. They understood Jebb's command and dragged the hefty body inside and rowed back towards their ship.

Jebb urged the men of Lindfield to clear the last piles on his part off the beach, ordered the landers to pull the Newhaven rowing boats up the beach, and turned for home well satisfied with the largest smuggling run the Ouse had ever known.

It was at this moment that one expected and one unexpected attack was made.

68

The Customs Officers arrived with raised guns as the Barcombe labourers were leaving Newhaven. There could be no fight. The Barcombe men were not armed. Their weapons were cudgels. The armed ruffians who would have protected them were now dispersed along the coast and up the Ouse. The Chief Customs Officer had two sets of instructions – one set from Customs House in London, and the other from Sir Charles Marsh in Newick. It was the latter set they obeyed.

The Customs Officers rounded the labourers up into a group. Four Customs Officers stood round them with raised guns. The discovery of a semi-conscious Eugene in one wagon surprised the Chief. He had imagined this troublesome parson was now either dead or on his way to France.

Eugene sat up, looked over the side of the wagon and focussed fuzzy eyes on the Chief.

'I congratulate you, sir,' he said in an uncertain voice. 'But you have caught innocent labourers and not the leaders, I can lead you to those.'

The Chief thought quickly.

'Do you know these men?'

'They are my parishioners.'

'If you can give me their names, I shall release them tonight and they must appear before the magistrate at Newick tomorrow.'

Eugene had never known such generosity, and promised he would see they appeared before the magistrate and that he would be there too.

The Chief was pleased too. No-one could blame him for relying on the church; he had not looked forward to keeping these surly looking men in captivity. But he had one more important task. He ordered his men to unload two large barrels from the last wagon.

'We shall keep these to test them and inform the magistrate. You may take the rest to Barcombe. We shall collect it later.'

The men of Barcombe and Eugene Chipperfield could not understand this. However, the Chief knew how much he was allowed, and he knew the danger if he were too greedy.

Eugene, though with an aching head and weak limbs after watching the Customs Officers take two barrels to their cart, said to Thomas Willis, 'You go on without me. Do not worry about the magistrate. I shall be there to protect you.'

And so the men of Barcombe headed off to Lewes through Piddinghoe and Rodmell, and Eugene slipped quietly into Newhaven still full of people and made for the cliff. Some musket shots startled him.

The charge of the Dragoons was not as successful as that of the Customs Officers. To start with they did not want to charge, and indeed twice refused to obey their Captain. However, by this time they had been discovered, possibly by the smugglers but more likely by the inhabitants of Newhaven. The soldiers crouching under the jetty with the water lapping at their feet were a wonderful target. There were plenty of round stones. Young and old had picked them up and hurled them under the jetty. This encouraged immediate obedience of the Captain's orders.

Out they sprang some with muskets raised and some with swords ready for plunging into someone.

'On to the beach,' shouted Captain Kay. 'Chase that boat.'

The soldiers intended to obey. However, they found running on round stones against the enemy and having a head still hazy from the hospitality of Newick were two obstacles. Fortunately for them the enemy had gone. Three musket shots rang out. Two were aimed at the sea, and one at the cliffs.

Jebb, who had just left the beach, ran into a soldier with a sword who had rushed off at right angles to the charge of the others.

He pinned the surprised Jebb against a wall.

'I've captured a smuggler, Captain,' shouted the delighted soldier.

Matthew called his men back and walked over without much hope expecting that the stupidest of his soldiers had probably captured the village parson.

Matthew looked at Jebb; Jebb looked at Matthew.

Captain Matthew Kay was disgusted with his part on the night of 14th January in Newhaven. However, as he awoke after an uncomfortable night in the Customs House at Newhaven, he consoled himself with the thought that he had captured one of the smugglers' leaders, Samuel Jebb. He knew that this chance capture probably meant the end of his army career but he had decided to end it anyway.

The Customs Officers had kept Samuel Jebb in captivity that night. Matthew did not know that the officers debated long whether to release him, but had finally decided that more glory and no less rewards would be gained by keeping him.

The Captain had sent his soldiers back to Newick at midnight with little sympathy about their complaints. Jebb, after swearing bitterly and cursing Kay had remained a model prisoner. The Customs Officers were happy to ensure that Jebb was handed over to the magistrate at Newick. Kay was surprised that Sir Charles Marsh was chosen by everybody. There was a Justice of the Peace at Lewes who was far closer, but as he knew Sir Charles, he was happy about the decision.

The Captain galloped quickly to Newick. He wanted to be there before Jebb.

While he galloped, George, Richard and Selina were still asleep. As George said later, 'It is strange what we are allowed to do when my parents are interested in something else.'

Eugene Chipperfield was also heading for Newick. He was walking. Farmer Cornwell's horse had had a hard night and deserved a rest.

Sir Adam was also up early. His labourers arrived at six o'clock, tired and dirty and full of worries about appearing before the magistrate. Sir Adam tried to reassure them. They still worried. They knew the punishments for smuggling. Hanging or transportation.

Sir Adam strolled round his grounds. His garden house was full of barrels; his farm barn was crammed with boxes. He smiled, looked at his motto and went inside for a brandy.

Sir Charles and Lady Marsh were eating breakfast when Eugene arrived. The Curate was asked to wait in Sir Charles's study while the knight finished his bread, butter and coffee. He asked for another cup. He was able, self-assured and yet cautious. As far as he knew the night had been a success; his one worry had been that Samuel Jebb had not reported to him. He knew the barns of Newick and, indeed Newick church were filled with unusual goods, which that day would be carried to London. He was not keen to see Eugene perhaps on some trivial church matter or on his complaints about the poverty of the labourers. However, it turned out to be neither. It was news he already knew.

'The labourers of Barcombe have been arrested for helping in smuggling and will be appearing before you,' said the Curate with new confidence. 'They are innocent parties in an evil game. I know the leader.'

'What? What's that, parson? The leader?'

'Yes, it is Samuel Jebb of the Sloop.'

'Ah, Jebb eh?' Sir Charles relaxed. 'I can tell you, parson, I have had my suspicions of Jebb for some time. In fact I sent that Captain of the Dragoons to watch him. I shall have him before me, parson. He will have to answer to the Justice of the Peace.'

'I had hoped for a judge and jury, for if I am right his sentence should be heavy.'

'My dear parson, you speak excellent legal sense. If the evidence is indeed strong and attested by many witnesses I should be the first to pass the case on to the assizes.'

With that there was an interruption. In came a dishevelled Captain Kay.

'Sir Charles,' he announced. 'I have arrested Samuel Jebb. He was smuggling on Newhaven beach last night and he should be arriving for an investigation by you and a transfer to the assizes.'

The Captain had no feelings of favour for the innkeeper who had led him from his duty deep into the paths of drink.

'Do not pre-suppose my judgement, Captain,' replied Sir Charles. 'I was just telling the parson I had chosen you to watch the innkeeper. I'm glad you have been worthy of my trust. I must ask you both to attend court this afternoon in which evidence will be heard. You may yourselves be required to give evidence. Captain Kay, see that Samuel Jebb and the accused labourers are brought to court at two o'clock.'

69

The court at Newick was Sir Charles's own hall. There was a dais at the end of it on which was a table with a carved chair beside it. In the hall were rows of benches and on the right hand side a wooden box four feet high with no ends and one side missing. This was for the accused to stand in.

The Dragoons, happy to be back in Newick and more sober than usual, were ushers. It seemed that the whole population of Barcombe and Newick was there. Every bench was filled and others stood round the side. Eugene was there, and so were Richard and Selina. George sat on a special chair by his father beside the dais.

Everyone stood up as Sir Charles Marsh entered. He was splendidly dressed in his largest, most frightening wig, a red coat trimmed with gold braid, a lace fronted shirt with frilly cuffs below the arms of the coat, blue trousers down to his knees up to which he had gold stockings. He motioned everyone to sit. How Sir Charles loved this.

He called the Newick Constable, Elias Rouse, who staggered up to him. Old age and blindness rather limited him, but he still had a loud voice.

'Call the Barcombe labourers,' he bellowed.

Two Dragoons led them in from a side room. The Constable pointed to the box for the defendants, but the efforts of the Dragoons to get six labourers into it, led to the fall of the box with a crash. The audience stirred and half cheered. Were the prisoners trying to break away? They were not. They stood dejected with bowed heads and thin faces. They were hungry and tired.

'Stand there,' shouted Rouse.

The Chief Customs Officer stood up and gave evidence against them.

'Why were you in Newhaven?' asked Sir Charles.

'We were given orders by . . . ' started Ebenezer.

Sir Charles interrupted him. 'What were your orders?'

'Sir Ad . . . '

'What were your orders?' shouted Sir Charles.

'To bring goods to the garden . . . '

'That is enough. Customs Officer!'

'Yes, sir,' replied the Customs Officer.

'Did you arrest these men on the beach?'

'No, sir. On the road to Lewes.'

'Did you see them on the beach?'

'No, sir.'

'Did you inspect their goods?'

'No, sir.'

'Thank you, Customs Officer. You have done an excellent job, which I shall make clear to the Customs House in London. I fear however we have not enough evidence with which to convict these undoubted scoundrels. I therefore dismiss the case!'

There were wild cheers from the audience and even Sir Adam smiled.

'Silence,' roared Constable Rouse. 'Call Samuel Jebb.'

At once the atmosphere grew tense as the feared, stocky, grim-faced innkeeper entered. The Dragoons got him successfully into the defendant's box.

'Captain Kay,' shouted the Constable to Kay who was just beside him. The Captain explained to Sir Charles how and where Jebb had been caught.

'Was Jebb on the beach when arrested?' asked Sir Charles.

'No, but he was only a few yards from it. He had . . . '

'Thank you, Captain. Now, Samuel Jebb, why were you in Newhaven.'

'I was visiting friends, sir,' he said in his usual surly voice.

'Friends? What friends? Are they here to give witness?'

'Yes,' said Jebb. 'It's the Customs Officers.'

Sir Charles did not seem surprised. The Constable staggered over and heard the magistrate's instructions.

'Call the Chief Customs Officer.'

The Customs Officer was all ready. He told Sir Charles that Jebb was an old friend to Customs Officials and had indeed called that night to warn them of a smuggling attempt.

'It seems he was right in that,' said Sir Charles laughing. 'I am most grateful to you Customs Officer. Your evidence has cleared the name of a man we know well in this district.'

As Samuel Jebb waited to be set free he had the greatest shock of his life. The man he had sent half dead to France the night before, stood up on the far side of the hall and, 'Wait, Sir Charles. You have been told lies. It's all lies. Samuel Jebb was on the beach . . . '

'Silence!' shouted Sir Charles loudly.

'Silence!' shouted Constable Rouse more loudly.

'I was there. I have already . . . '

'Sit down, sir. You have not been called as a witness. Samuel Jebb, you are free.'

'Sir, I demand to be heard,' shouted Eugene. The crowd, smugglers all, hated Samuel Jebb. They did not shout Eugene down, but Sir Charles shouted.

'Carry him away, Dragoons. He will be arrested if he talks again.'

The Dragoons grabbed Eugene. Richard beside him shouted, 'He's telling the truth, we saw it all.'

Richard was knocked down by another Dragoon and carried out.

George ran to the front. 'I saw Samuel Jebb with the smugglers. He was . . . '

His father grabbed him from behind, and pulled him gasping and shouting away.

'Chastise your son severely,' shouted the annoyed Sir Charles. 'The court is closed.'

'The court is closed,' yelled Constable Rouse.

EPILOGUE

Thus our story ends. Perhaps we can look ahead a year or two later with some of the characters.

Captain Clow and the princess were not as successful as they had planned. Though they traded slaves for a few years they did not become rich. Captain Clow died and the princess returned to her tribe.

The large Herbert Jenkins married the ugly Pamela Horspool and with the help of John Wesley took over the Foundlings' Home from the Shillibeers. What a happy couple they were, and what a happy home it was, and none was happier there than Joanna, Mark and Simon.

The Shillibeers returned to Newick, where they knew they would find a good job. Edmund was perhaps the only man in the world who had Sir Charles under his thumb. Sir Charles, in spite of this, continued to be a prosperous gentleman and magistrate. News of the court case did spread to London, but a conversation with the Duke of Newcastle allayed any troubles.

Captain Matthew Kay left the Army and began training as a lawyer. After the court case in Newick he realized some honest lawyers were needed.

Eugene's popularity with the people of Barcombe saved him from fleeing from Sussex as any other informer about smuggling had to do. At Sarah's suggestion and with Sarah's money he started a school for all in a great barn at Barcombe Cross. Sir Adam would not have allowed George to go to a school with labourers' children, but everybody else overruled him, even Lady Katharine.

Sir Adam was still a mixture of contentment and anxiety. He was rich after the successful smuggling run from Newhaven, but no more was coming in. Strangely, Eugene Chipperfield had put paid to large scale smuggling up the Ouse for many years. Sarah's coming to Kilmore House meant generous help from her; on the other hand she had insisted that he doubled the wages of all his workers.

Sarah had sold her house in Whitechapel, closed the slave-trading company, and began a new company with her two ships. This time the ships carried goods and not people for sale. She introduced her two Johns, Blackman and Wesley to each other.

Shortly afterwards the Rector of Barcombe came to live in Barcombe. He could never forget the story of Cognatus that Sarah had told him. He visited the labourers and followed Eugene's example of helping them when in need. He was still in love with Sarah.

George and Richard were good friends. Their adventures at Newhaven and Newick made a link between them that was not to be broken.

Richard enjoyed life at Kilmore House, school with Eugene, whom he admired very much, and one day he was going to meet Captain Cripps again.

Selina too was happy, loved school and one day was going to meet again the first man she loved, John Newton. It was going to be a very different John Newton then.

Richard and Selina were orphans but they had a new mother now, the lovely, laughing Sarah.